Victorian Visionary

The Art of
Elliott Daingerfield

Neptune's Daughter, c. 1913-1915, Oil on canvas, 24 x 34 ¼ inches, 1993.C0735

VICTORIAN VISIONARY

The Art of Elliott Daingerfield

Essays by
ESTILL CURTIS PENNINGTON
and
J. RICHARD GRUBER

with a foreword by
WILLIAM S. MORRIS III

MORRIS MUSEUM OF ART
Augusta, Georgia

1994

The authors gratefully acknowledge the assistance of Catherine W. Wahl in the preparation of this publication, and thank Lydia Inglett and Vincent Bertucci for the catalogue design which captures the spirit of Daingerfield and his era.

CIP 93-080647 / ISBN 0-9638753-2-9

CONTENTS

VII

FOREWORD
William S. Morris III

11

SOUTHERN FIRES, NORTHERN LIGHTS
The Southern life and Northern journey of Elliott Daingerfield
as found in his autobiographical fragments
Estill Curtis Pennington

17

ELLIOTT DAINGERFIELD AND THE SYMBOLIST SPIRIT 1893–1916
J. Richard Gruber

53

CHECKLIST OF THE DAINGERFIELD COLLECTION

67

INDEX OF ILLUSTRATIONS

FOREWORD

The art of Elliott Daingerfield and the evolution of his career, stretching from his roots in the South of the Confederacy to his rise as a major artist in the New York art world, constitute one of the most intriguing chapters in the history of the art of the South. Even at the peak of his accomplishments in the art centers of the North, Daingerfield remained directly connected to the culture, history and environment of the South.

His vision was not limited by the realm of the academic art world nor was it confined to the geography of the North or the South.

With this catalogue, and the exhibition it accompanies, the Morris Museum of Art hopes to bring the art of Elliott Daingerfield to a new generation of museum visitors and to contribute, as well, to the growing research on the artist which has appeared in recent years. More than twenty years ago, in 1971, Cleve Scarbrough and Robert Hobbs organized a major retrospective exhibition of Daingerfield's art at the Mint Museum of Art in Charlotte. In the intervening years, Daingerfield, like many important academic artists working in America at the turn of the century, has received renewed recognition.

The Morris Museum of Art feels a particular obligation to contribute to this growing interest and dialogue on the artist and to the larger context of painting in the South and in America at the turn of the century. The Daingerfield holdings in the museum's permanent collection, consisting of over one hundred paintings and works on paper, constitute the largest body of work by a single artist in our permanent collection and, we believe, the largest collection of his works in any public institution. We are indebted to the late Dr. Robert Powell Coggins, whose tireless collecting efforts and unflagging interest in the career of Daingerfield contributed to the foundation of the collection.

Born in Harper's Ferry on the eve of the Civil War, Daingerfield was raised as the son of a Confederate Army officer in Fayetteville, North Carolina. Suffering the deprivations so commonly evident in the South during the era of Reconstruction, Daingerfield ventured north in 1880 to fulfill his dream of becoming an artist in New York. By 1886, when he set up his first studio in Blowing Rock, North Carolina, he had established the two centers for his personal life and his professional career. Daingerfield established a significant reputation as an academic artist and as a Symbolist painter during a vital time in the evolution of American art.

Daingerfield's roots in the South and his early years in New York are well considered in the following essay by Estill Curtis Pennington, Curator of Southern Painting at the Morris Museum. In his accompanying essay, J. Richard Gruber, Deputy Director of the Museum, examines Daingerfield's years as a Symbolist painter and places him in the larger context of national and international Symbolist directions.

Elliott Daingerfield is often called the most important artist of North Carolina. We hope that this exhibition helps to bring the artist to greater recognition in the South and beyond for contemporary audiences.

–WILLIAM S. MORRIS III
Chairman, Board of Trustees

Kenyon Cox – Portrait of Elliott Daingerfield, *1890, Oil on canvas, 20 x 16 inches, 1993.C0079*

SOUTHERN FIRES, NORTHERN LIGHTS

The Southern life and Northern journey of Elliott Daingerfield as found in his autobiographical fragments

*A*ny considered approach to the life and art of Elliott Daingerfield must begin in the South, where the artist's formative years, as recorded in his earnestly Victorian autobiographical jottings, set a distinctive tone and tenor for his entire life. As he, himself, wrote, consideration of Elliott Daingerfield's art must begin "with its origin and his own equipment and his own ambitions."

Daingerfield's family history combines the local gentry of the valley of Virginia with an outcrossing of Huguenot immigrants. Daingerfield's mother, a de Brua, was as he notes, called simply "Brua." His father was always distinctly proud of the family's Virginia heritage, so much so that long after they had moved to North Carolina he forbade the young Daingerfield to even think of travelling through the Old Dominion without stopping repeatedly to visit distant relatives and share the well known hospitality of the area.

Daingerfield's father was taken hostage by the abolitionist John Brown at Harper's Ferry in 1859, and held against his will until forces under the command of Robert E. Lee put an end to the uprising. "It is always a pleasure to me," Daingerfield wrote, "to know that when Col. Lee came with Government troops to quell that rising, he made my father's house his headquarters and I was many times in his arms, being the baby of the family."

After he was cradled in the nursery of secession and war, Daingerfield and his family moved south to Fayetteville, North Carolina, where Daingerfield's father took charge of yet another arsenal. That home provided the artist's first memories, an archetypal setting redolent of Southern mythic longings. "Memory, I am told, of these early days is hardly possible, but nevertheless I well remember the first house we lived in – its stately columns – its iron fence and general spaciousness."

While the family's residence was of short duration, it and the events of the war, were burned into Daingerfield's mind. "It was a time of great tenseness, great emotions, great privations, great poverty – each one a hot iron to sear the soul and keep memory alive." Much of his formative life was spent escaping the death and destruction which the privations of the War between the States visited upon the citizenry as well as the forces in the field.

He saw his mother feed young Confederate officers "in tattered clothes and starved" at a table which could scarcely provide for the inhabitants of a house deserted by adult males and kept going by the ceaseless energies of stalwart women and resourceful children. He watched in horror as Union forces evacuated his family from their home prior to burning it down. A treasured wine bottle and an heirloom gun were damaged by the invading soldiers. The wine bottle was to have been Daingerfield's first prized possession. The damaged gun, with associations to George Washington and his family, remained with him for the rest of his life. Reconstruction also proved daunting for the family of a Confederate veteran. Although his father and brother returned from the front unharmed, there was no money and little food. During this time he remembered his mother's "courage and calm, and her willingness to do whatever could be done." With ingenuity and imagination they survived in palmetto hats and clothing made from old table linens, using poke berries for ink.

Young Elliott records episodes of racial hatred and violent resistance to assimilation during those days when the Freedman's Bureau dominated the political process of every Southern state. He witnessed a lynching, and heard the shots which ended, in death, the bitter argument between an esteemed local veteran and a despised official of occupation forces. "The times," he wrote, "were dreadful and the conditions worse."

But never does he suggest that life was too harsh for him. His father had opened a store and the family moved to a house on a "broad sheet of water, backed up by the town mill-dam. It was a lovely place for boating, and at night the young people rowed and drifted about, singing the old Southern songs which to me, lying in bed and listening, were very dear." He felt these songs were "wonderful, and the impression is still very vivid in my memory."

In the midst of this most quintessential of Southern exposures, Daingerfield discovered that he wanted to be an artist. Not terribly interested in sports, he learned the rudiments of carpentry work from two old black cabinetmakers. And then his brother, Archie, brought home "equipment he had bought and the use of which he had been taught by an itinerant, ..." a statement that affirms the enduring legacy of that artistic tradition.

At first he copied old prints and illustrations from *Godey's Ladies Book*. Then he joined forces with a sign painter, "a good looking devil who drank too much," and learned the craft. From this sign painter Daingerfield also learned the basics of modeling and depth and perspective, energetically and profitably pursuing the painting of signs and making his first attempts at art.

His longing heart, however, was "filled with the wish to do better things – pictures in fact." To do so he solicited the help of a local lady, one Mrs. McKay, who taught all she knew of composition and coloration. To the mind of a twelve year old, "it was a message straight out of heaven. The very smell of paint was a joy."

Even as he grew in craft, he realized the limitations of the locale. The would-be artist saw public executions, ran with local militia companies and met his first proper young ladies, whose company excited him to blush. He continued to paint, and to begin dreaming of a career in the north. His "heart and mind were set on New York. If anywhere, there was the chance for an artistic career," and he began saving up funds to make the journey north toward this fabled centrist locale and formal art study.

From his recollections we gather that he was already beginning to paint works with a mystical, symbolic meaning. Many, he recalls, were of Madonnas or weeping Magdalenes. One particularly ambitious work was of a baby attempting to nurse at the breast of its dead mother – tribute to an epidemic story – which he notes "oblivion has kindly overtaken."

Interestingly enough, nowhere in these early reminiscences is there any mention of his participation in organized religion. He does make frequent mention of faith, and of his parents' emphasis on good values and moral teachings. It seems a subtle reminder that the fervid fundamentalist orgies of the second quarter of the nineteenth century South, the South of the great revivals, had died down into a kind of benign genteel acceptance of good form. In the not too distant future the fervor of fundamentalism would return with baptisms of fire and blood, but in Daingerfield's youth a certain quiet deism held ground.

It is, then, all the more fascinating that Daingerfield had one of his first mystical revelations while still a youth in Fayetteville. While with a group of his fellows out in the country on a fishing trip he was caught in a storm.

The vividness of the lightening was intense. We stopped for an instant to watch it, when suddenly that great purple cloud rolled away, or rather, seemed to open – behind it standing quietly was a figure, majestic, calm and very gracious – the hair was in long curly billows about the face, the face itself turned full upon us looked out from great eyes. The costume was simple and long, and we knew the figure at once and were terrified. The figure of the Savior! There could be no mistake. It was not an illusion made by cloud forms as we often see in the sky. All about it was an intense light, and the figure was in violet half-tone.

Although this was an incident which Daingerfield claimed he "never understood … nor has anyone explained" it was obviously a shaping moment in his mystical understanding of the forces of nature and art, his greatest theme in maturity. Much later in his life, he reported, Albert Pinkham Ryder, the American symbolist master, "begged me to paint it," but he felt he could not. Even so, the setting of his work *The Mystic Brim*, with the figure of great authority poised on the right side of the picture plane, at least echoes this Southern revelation.

Daingerfield glimpsed the Savior near the time he realized his days in the South were

drawing to a close. His mind "was made up – for New York to make or break in the life I wished." After the predictable shocking confrontations with his family, in which the male members disapproved of his endeavors even as his mother encouraged him and gave him such small financial aid as she could, he set out.

Daingerfield's vision of New York as a celestial haven for the sanctification of artistic ambition was based on certain rudimentary correspondence he had conducted with various galleries and dealers there. Certainly the city had a long tradition of artistic success, dating back to the times of Thomas Cole and the founding of the American Art-Union and the National Academy of Design. What Daingerfield hoped to find was further instruction, a market for his works, and acceptance into the hallowed hall of the National Academy of Design.

His move to the "far-off North where I was to make a place for myself" offers a rather engaging parable in the passage of a young man from a shabby genteel background in the South making a transition to a worldly, and oft-times overwhelming major urban area. And though this passage is not unlike the transition experienced by other American picaresque characters forging the same trail of assimilation and success, it is underlaid with the subtle tones of a Southerner who knows good form, and whose self-confidence proceeds from the prevailing Southern values of the time.

Quite abruptly, Daingerfield's life shifts from the quiet, relative warmth, both social and climatic, of the rural South, to the surging, bustling cold of a northern urban winter. Though frightened and "green," Daingerfield resolves to stay on course, fighting his way through the crowds from the ferry boat to the dock, salvaging his luggage and managing to get himself across the city to a boarding house.

His written record of these days would seem to indicate that an unquestioning belief in the resources of his Southern identity stood him in good stead at almost every turn. In the boarding house luncheon room, "the negro waiter knew me as a Southerner and was most attentive," bringing his first meal, even as he was writing his mother of "a room so small I had to go outside to change my expression."

Immediately he set about to use his Southern manners to ease his loneliness and sustain him against the fears of the city. Predictably enough he found the Northerners in his boarding house to be cold and aloof, never speaking at dinner. He observed to his fellow boarders that he was "not accustomed to meals in silence," and made conversation. The dining room thawed under the inspiration of his folksy Southern ways and "people even laughed and became human."

Like the charming hero of an apologist novel of manners, Daingerfield tacked between the ports of Southern innocence and northern experience. Everywhere he went, his polite Southern upbringing was a help. When he presented himself to an artist, Walter Satterlee, for apprenticeship, the old painter asked, "are you Daingerfield from Virginia?" When he replied that indeed he was, the artist took him in and gave him work, setting him further on the course to being a full-fledged painter.

Although given aid by his father's sister's husband, a wealthy financier, he was taken aback by the sumptuous manner in which they lived. "My bringing up in a village during wartime poverty had taught me nothing of such surroundings and habits of life." But he remained undaunted, going about the city on long walks, taking in such exalted social occasions as his genteel connections permitted, and diligently pursuing his course as an artist in the making.

There were setbacks, both curious and comical. He was refused admission to a high Episcopal Church because he was not dressed properly, his first experience, as a white man, with discrimination not based on race, but on class. He was reminded by several acquaintances, that in New York, "men are judged by the clothes they wear." Ultimately, his wealthy relations provided him with the proper attire, and though grateful, he pondered the meaning of artifice over sincerity. Shockingly enough, he concluded that "people prefer a man in good clothes rather than one with a clean heart."

The New York which Daingerfield was coming to know was the New York of Henry James and Edith Wharton, the New York in which lingering Knickerbocker gentility was being swept aside by the robber baron plutocracy. It was a New York in which political rings conspired to keep political power in the city out of the hands of the immigrants and the labor class. Increasingly the South was shut out of national political life and left alone, in the aftermath of the compromises following the disputed election of 1876, to overthrow disastrous reconstruction policies, settling in to the reactionary spirit of Bourbon agrarianism.

Through this world Daingerfield moved, if not with ease, at least with the armor of his Southern heritage. He often amused his northern hostesses with stories of his Southern home, dining out on tales of endurance and remote country charm. At times hungry, and certainly at times quite lonely, he remained determined to be an artist. The autobiographical fragments end just as Daingerfield is beginning to enjoy his first success as a painter. He has a work accepted for the juried show at the National Academy of Design, and makes his first big sale.

At this point no subsequent chapters of Daingerfield's autobiography have come to light. There is, therefore, a lamentable gap between his self-confessed progress as a pilgrim in search of art education, and his great personal successes in the last years of the nineteenth century. One longs to read of his first meetings with George Inness, who would have such a profound influence upon his life and art. Or, for that matter, to know of his feeling about Albert Pinkham Ryder, Ralph Blakelock, and the expatriate giants with whom he came in contact.

Even without the words, the spirit and tone of the early reminiscences surely provide the palette with which any further recollections would be colored. In Daingerfield's voice we can just hear the echo of a very Southern sense of self, rising from the ashes of war with poetic resolve, lingering through the time obsessed fantasies which echo in the writings of William

Faulkner and Tennessee Williams until they play out in the modern grotesque of Flannery O'Connor and Peter Taylor.

Elliott Daingerfield's being was formed by a first-hand knowledge of the loss and suffering caused by a great and tragic war. He grew up with a profound sense of place, heightened by his rambles through the countryside, to which, after all, he would return, building a Southern studio in which he painted some of his greatest landscape art. From his family he learned an innate sense of good form, manners which gave him the courage to confront those far superior in wealth, but much less empowered in good graces.

Ultimately, he came to the conclusion that "the province of the artist being to express the beautiful," he had a mission, which, if not divine, was at least mystical. This belief cannot be laid entirely at the feet of the Southern altar of good form. It reeks of the kind of high Victorian idealism propagated by John Ruskin and William Morris; the ideal, in Daingerfield's words, that "art which is immortal renders a people immortal."

Sifting through the remains of Daingerfield's artistic material culture, we are left to ponder his Southern landscapes, his grand ladies of the canyons, perched somewhat precariously above their imaginary terrain, and his astonishingly accomplished drawings. Pausing to contemplate their worth and place we might do well to consider the early years, when yet one more Southern boy journeyed out of the fire of a Southern sunset toward the lights of a Northern city to find, if not acclaim, at least the full expression of a powerful imagination.

– ESTILL CURTIS PENNINGTON

FOOTNOTES

1. All quotes taken from "Autobiography of Elliott Daingerfield," a rough typescript of which was given to the late Dr. Robert Powell Coggins of Marietta, Georgia in the early 1980s. When the Coggins collection came into the possession of the Morris Museum of Art in 1989, this typescript was part of the transferred manuscript collection, and is now in the Daingerfield Papers at the Center for the Study of Southern Painting at the Morris Museum of Art in Augusta, Georgia. Most of this same manuscript is also on microfilm at the Archives of American Art, Smithsonian Institution, Washington, D.C.

2. Charles Bracelen Flood. *Lee: The Last Years*. Boston, 1981, p. 237.

Illustration 1–Self Portrait, c. 1890, Oil on canvas, 28⅛ x 24¹/₁₀ inches, 1993.C0313

"Art is the principle flowing out of God
through certain men and women,
by which they perceive and understand the beautiful.
Sculpture, architecture, pictures, and music
are the languages of the spirit."

– Elliott Daingerfield[1]

"If one were to ask Mr. Daingerfield
what is most essential [in the art of painting]…
he would say to you 'spiritual vision.'
This is sometimes called merely imagination.
It is something higher than that, says Mr. Daingerfield.
Spiritual vision is a message imparted to a man of genius who,
if he has the technical ability, may pass it on to the observer…
It is the light of the spirit, the presence of the something
which has no material or objective expression."

– Elliott Daingerfield[2]

ELLIOTT DAINGERFIELD AND THE SYMBOLIST SPIRIT 1893–1916

In an early self-portrait, completed in 1890, a serious and self-confident Elliott Daingerfield looks directly at the viewer with a searching gaze (*illustration 1*). The mood and the tones of the painting are dark, suggesting age, a patina of history and, perhaps, a degree of experience beyond the artist's years. At the age of 31, Elliott Daingerfield had achieved a certain level of recognition in the New York art world.

Just ten years earlier he had arrived in the city as an unknown. He had travelled to New York from his home in North Carolina, intent upon becoming a professional artist. Raised in Fayetteville, the son of the commander of the Confederate Arsenal there, he was left with an indelible connection to the history, culture and environment of the region of his birth. The challenges of his youth in the South also nurtured Daingerfield's sense of determination and his sense of vision. From an early age, and continuing throughout his career as an American painter, Daingerfield possessed the ability to see beyond surfaces, to see beyond the immediate world around him. He was driven to seek deeper truths and to paint works which reflected his belief in "spiritual vision."

Throughout his career, Daingerfield's art and aesthetic philosophy reflected a strong connection to the sensitivities and spirit of the South. If the South was the land of his birth and his early development, the art world of Manhattan would provide the setting for his professional maturation. From the time of this self-portrait until his death in 1932, Daingerfield maintained studios and residences in both New York City and Blowing Rock, North Carolina. His artistic talents and his aesthetic vision were nurtured by the very different atmospheres of both locales. This became particularly evident in the years from 1893 to 1916 when Daingerfield's art merged a series of diverse national and international influences to create a distinctive body of work.

The paintings created in these years, particularly the Symbolist images, are the subject of this essay. The evolution of his work in the years from 1880 to 1916 will be considered in

Illustration 2 – Lady with Flower - Nude Study, no date, Graphite on paperboard, 15⅝ x 11⅞ inches, 1993.C0895

the context of three related periods. The first, dating from 1880 to about 1892, reflected his immersion in the advanced art world of New York, his exposure to academic systems and his personal experiences in the company of such influential artists as George Inness and Albert Pinkham Ryder. The second, from 1893 to 1910, marks his maturation as a painter, his development as a successful artist and the evolution of his early Symbolist period. Finally, in the years from 1910 to 1916, he reached the peak of his Symbolist activities, culminating in his most imaginative and visionary efforts, the paintings of the West and the Grand Canyon.

Some of his paintings exist beyond these general classifications. However, because the issues he explored flowed continually forward, it will become apparent that the art of Elliott Daingerfield was created in a systematic, methodical and distinctly evolutionary process. All of the paintings and works on paper discussed, unless otherwise identified, are drawn from the extensive Daingerfield holdings now contained in the permanent collections of the Morris Museum of Art. Photographs, estate papers and artist's journals referred to in this essay are included in the Daingerfield collections of the Center for the Study of Southern Painting at the Morris Museum of Art.

DAINGERFIELD AS THE "AMERICAN MILLET"

Elliott Daingerfield described his earliest years in an understated way: "He received a common school education in a small town and began working for himself at a very early age, always however with the idea of one day taking up art as a profession. He went to New York when he was about twenty-one years of age and met all the difficulties and trials that a young man without money, without acquaintance or friends would meet in a great city."[3] In the South of his youth, torn by the Civil War and the burdens of Reconstruction, there had been only limited opportunities to study art. His own experience there included training in china painting and in commercial photography. By 1880, when he arrived in New York, he would discover that major changes were occurring in urban America and in the American art world. As recently as 1875, for example, there had been only ten art schools in the country. By 1882, nurtured in part by the popularity of American art during the centennial year, particularly at the Philadelphia Centennial Exposition of 1876, the number had grown to thirty-nine art schools.[4] Daingerfield entered the realm of academic art during a period of unprecedented interest and expansion in America.

Daingerfield would also learn that the artists of his age sought to distance themselves from the styles and philosophies of the older generation. Henry Adams, one of his contemporaries, placed emphasis upon the "generation of 1870" and the importance of the year 1870 as a cultural milestone: "The generation that lived from 1840 to 1870 could do very well with the old forms of education; that which had its work to do between 1870 and 1900 needed something quite new."[5] For these younger artists the influences of painting and art training in Paris and Munich were critical. An emphasis upon academic systems, including the study of the nude model, immersion in technique and the study of art history, were increasingly evident.[6] The hegemony of the Hudson River School was passing. The more subtle and subjective influences of the French Barbizon School were on the ascendancy. As American artists traveled and studied in France and Italy, the paintings and techniques of Renaissance artists also exerted an increasing influence upon American art and academic training. Contemporary writers and later historians often identified the period as the "American Renaissance."

Daingerfield's connection to the academic system began shortly after his arrival in

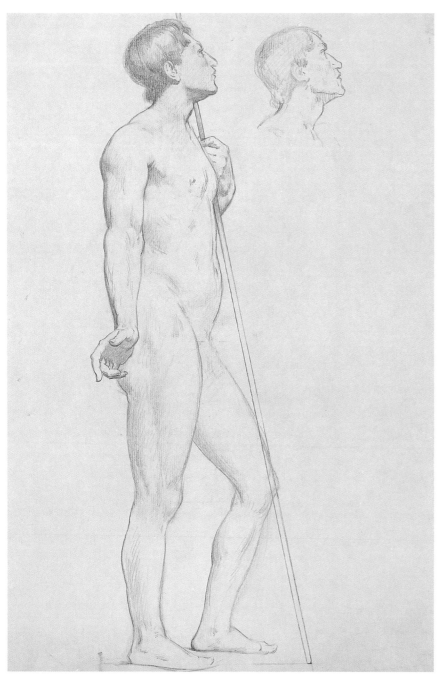

Illustration 3 –Archangel Michael - Nude Study B, 1902-1906, Graphite on paper, 19½ x 15½ inches, 1993.C0919

New York when he became a studio assistant to Walter Satterlee, who was at that time an associate member of the National Academy of Design. As evidence of his aptitude and his awareness of these academic directions, Daingerfield became an instructor in Satterlee's life class, a position he retained for four years. Before the end of this first year in New York he also exhibited a painting, *The Monk Smelling a Bottle of Wine*, at the National Academy of Design.[7] Daingerfield immersed himself in the life of the New York art world in these years. While teaching with Satterlee he enrolled in classes at the Art Students League. Established in 1875, it incorporated the theories and techniques then evident in the French academies. Influential teachers, including Kenyon Cox, who became a friend and professional colleague of Daingerfield, maintained the dominance of the French schools at the League. During these years Daingerfield established his proficiency in drawing and demonstrated increasing talent in the presentation of the academic nude.

Two notable events, both occurring in 1884, added increased direction to his personal life and his professional career. First, he married Roberta Strange French, the daughter of a judge from Wilmington, North Carolina. The importance of her family connections reinforced his own ties to the life and traditions of the South. In the fall he moved to the Holbein Studios, located on Fifty-fifth street. Here he met George Inness, one of the most important and successful painters of the period. Inness served as a leading proponent of the French Barbizon ideals and advocated a more subjective attitude toward the American landscape than that of the earlier Hudson River School painters.[8] Daingerfield later remembered that this "was the real starting point of the artist's development… not a day passed that he did not watch Mr. Inness at work or have visits from the master in his studio, with criticisms of his own work."[9] In turn, Inness praised the younger artist's talents and encouraged his patrons to buy Daingerfield's paintings.

Important aesthetic and intellectual bonds were formed in the Holbein

Studios. Inness introduced Daingerfield to members of the city's artistic and intellectual elite. Trends in art, literature and philosophy were discussed, often reflecting international concerns about the booming financial and industrial development evident in America and France. "In their postwar booms," Charles Eldredge observes," America and France, and indeed much of Europe, saw traditional values being threatened by the rampant materialism which accompanied economic growth" contributing to the development of the Symbolist mood in France and the Genteel Tradition and Idealism in America. "By whatever name, the flourishing of idealism and introspective imagination at the end of the nineteenth century was decidedly international in scope, and paralleled the romantic response of nearly a century earlier."[10] Daingerfield, deeply affected by his early experiences in the South and interested in the relationship between the spiritual and art, found much to consider in these developments, including Inness's immersion in the theories and philosophies of Emmanuel Swedenborg, an eighteenth-century Swedish theologian who enjoyed a notable revival in America after the Civil War.[11]

In 1886, while still absorbing these influences, he first ventured to Blowing Rock. Searching initially for an environment in which to recover from diptheria, Daingerfield found a Southern retreat where he could also continue his spiritual and aesthetic explorations. Here, in the mountains of North Carolina, he recovered his physical health and, at the same time, also discovered the source for much of his continuing artistic inspiration. The discovery of Blowing Rock completed a creative circle for Daingerfield. With the intellectual and artistic stimulation available at his New York studio, and the tranquility of his summer residence in the Blue Ridge Mountains, the artist had found the sites and inspiration which would govern the annual cycles of his artistic and personal life. A painting completed in 1886, *Chrysanthemums in a Devil Vase (illustration 4)* demonstrates how focused his artistic goals were by this time. An accomplished and confident painting, the composition fills the picture plane with a cascade of brilliantly painted flowers spilling from the upper left corner of the canvas downward in an arcing curve to the surface of the polished table. The

Illustration 4 – Chrysanthemums in a Devil Vase , 1886 , Oil on canvas, 34 x 24 inches, 1989.01.048

Illustration 5 – Return at Twilight, 1887, Oil on canvas, 28⅛ x 48⅛ inches, 1989.01.047

use of a richly colored, dark background, similar to that of the *Self-Portrait* of 1890, offers a dramatic contrast to the bright coloration of the floral composition.

In *Return at Twilight*, painted in 1887, the influence of Inness, in subject, mood and tone, is quite evident (*illustration 5*). Under the glow of a rising moon, a peasant woman returns home through a pasture leading a flock of geese. The geese subtly take on the reflective tone of the moon adding a warm glow to the surface of the painting. Its quiet, introspective quality, and its reference to the subjects and mood of the Barbizon School, reflect the growing fascination with French art. It also shows the movement away from the detailed and often grandiose landscapes of the Hudson River School. A later painting, *Milk*

Maid (*illustration 6*) shows his continuing interest in relating the influences of Inness and the Barbizon School to the American aesthetic. His mastery of the Barbizon style demonstrates why he acquired a reputation in some circles as "the American Millet."[12]

An intimate painting of 1887, *Steeplechase*, continues the mood and tonalities of these two works but suggests the influence of a different, more uniquely American aesthetic upon Daingerfield (*illustration 7*). Living in New York, with ties to leading figures in the progressive art world, Daingerfield could not have escaped an awareness of the art of Albert Pinkham Ryder. Ryder's small, expressionistic landscapes were being championed by many in the city's avant garde when Daingerfield arrived in New York. If not learned directly from

Inness, he would have seen an obvious connection to some of Inness's sources because Ryder also reflected the influence of the Barbizon School in America. The paintings of Ryder would have been available to Daingerfield privately and through exhibitions. Ryder, who was elected to membership in the newly formed Society of American Artists in 1878, exhibited annually with this group from 1878 to 1884. By the time of Daingerfield's *Steeplechase*, Ryder had executed some of his most important paintings: *Jonah*, painted in 1885; *The Temple of the Mind*, completed in 1887 and *The Flying Dutchman*, exhibited in 1887 and the subject of excellent reviews in the major New York papers.[13]

Ryder's early paintings were influential at the time, as Elizabeth Broun concludes, because they offered a vision of the American landscape far removed from the style, and the intent, of earlier American landscape painting. "He did not depict the natural wonders of Niagara or Yellowstone, which Americans considered their divine endowment… Ryder's landscapes played to no such national agenda." They were, instead, much closer to a contemporary spirit and vision: "They were emblems of something private or internal, something that authors of the day liked to call 'poetic' because it worked through analogy or reference. Ryder's landscapes evoke a state of mind, one that entered the American consciousness with the disillusionment that followed the Civil War…"[14] Barbara Novak has compared Ryder to Thomas Cole, who once complained of America's devotion to "things, not thought." Ryder, she observes "can be said to have made thought into a thing" and because of his understanding that a painting is a "self-contained structure, an autonomous object" she finds Ryder to be "more genuinely a part of the international developments of his age" than other American artists of his time.[15] To many of his contemporaries, Ryder's isolation from the public mainstream, his eccentric manners and his rejection of the materialistic goals of the era were viewed as signs of his stature as a "true" artist, not unlike the romantic aesthetes emerging in France.

Like Ryder, Daingerfield came to value the autonomous existence of each painting. The dark shadows in *Steeplechase*, and the contrasting use of light upon the small, fleeting horses in the middle ground, suggest a sense of abstract composition, a minimal depiction of

Illustration 6 – Milk Maid, 1890-1910, Oil on canvas, 24 x 34 inches, 1989.01.041

Illustration 7 – Steeplechase, 1887, Oil on canvas, 7 x 9⅛ inches, 1989.01.050

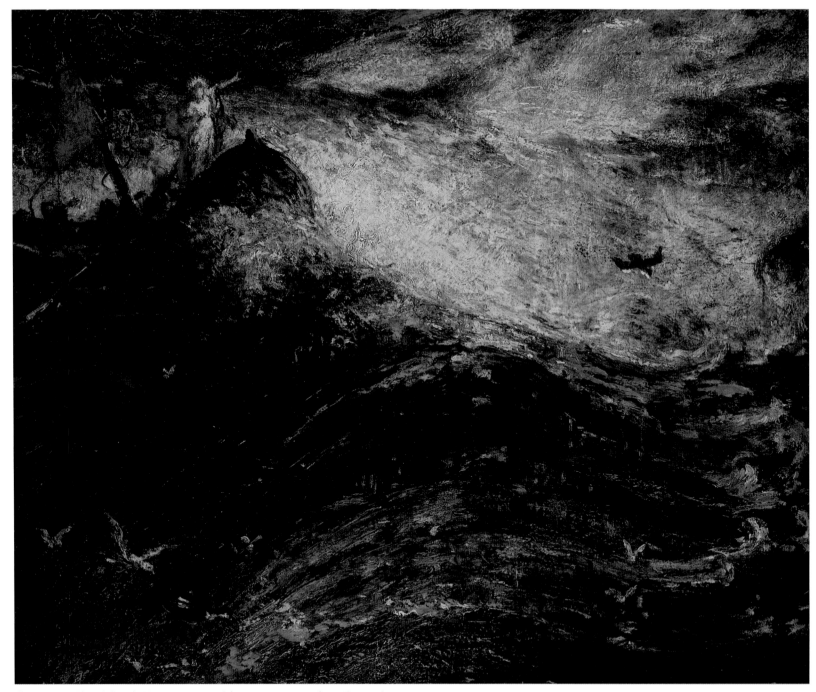

Illustration 8 – Christ Stilling the Tempest, 1905-10, Oil on canvas, 20 x 24 inches, 1989.01.046

an actual chase through the woods. The visual impression, the uses of color and the patterns of light become more important than the subject of the title. Daingerfield met Ryder and became personally acquainted with his aesthetic philosophies. Later in his career, when Daingerfield established a reputation as a serious and respected critic, he wrote that Ryder "preferred the terms of true poesy, the privilege of awakening the highest imagination… Fact did not interest him—truth and beauty did."[16] Those same interests came to have an increasing influence in Daingerfield's own paintings of these years.

A more direct relationship to Ryder's painting can be found in Daingerfield's *Christ Stilling the Tempest* (1905-1910). In subject, in mood and in coloration, his continuing debt to Ryder is particularly evident in this work (*illustration 8*). By the mid 1890s, Daingerfield's art reflected a deep and direct concern with religious and spiritual themes, including a desire to illustrate key passages from the Gospels. The seriousness of the artist's intent has been suggested by Robert Hobbs: "According to his daughters, Daingerfield hung in his studio a large crucifix from Salisbury Cathedral. Before he began to paint, this artist would kneel in front of the cross in prayer. He expressed in these prayers the desire to produce pictures which would inspire the highest good."[17] Daingerfield admired Ryder's approach to the portrayal of religious themes including his painting of Jonah which he described as a "dramatic vision" and a "high plane of interpretive art." Writing about *Jonah* after the death of Ryder in 1918, Daingerfield observed that in this painting the "sense of the storm in the lashing waters and the flying clouds is impressive, but Ryder contrives in all he does to secure by means wholly his own the presence of the mysterious."[18] This description might apply equally well to Daingerfield's own *Christ Stilling the Tempest*.

SYMBOLIST DIRECTIONS AND *THE MYSTIC BRIM*

The established rhythms and order of Daingerfield's life were severely disrupted in 1891. As a result, his paintings began to reflect a different vision, one which brought the artist closer to the concerns of Symbolist painters and poets then working in America and Europe. This change was initiated by the loss of his wife, Roberta, who died during childbirth. The profound loss and sadness which accompanied this event contributed to the beginning of an even deeper level of introspection and speculation about the realms of the spiritual and the afterlife. In *The Mystic Brim,* painted in 1893, Daingerfield portrayed the transition to the afterlife in a visionary work of notable power (*illustration 9*). Standing on the edge of a precipice, two figures, wrapped in robes and classical attire, look toward a bright and powerful swirling form filled with the suggestion of spirits. A protective angel hovers behind them.[19] Like a number of artists at the turn of the century, including Ryder, he composed poems to accompany his most important works.

Two years after her death, Daingerfield addressed the loss of his wife in a painting that is a forceful and distinctive work. It also offers a decidedly optimistic view, portraying as it does, the entrance to the afterlife as an environment of light and swirling forms of energy. The passage, the spiritual transition from one life to another, is presented as a bright, mysterious venture of faith and the ultimate reward for a life well lived. In *The Mystic Brim* he blends a theme of strong personal and emotional interest with his academic background, his figurative skills and his interest in allegory to achieve a unique transcendental image. *The Mystic Brim* offers a notable contrast to the monument Henry Adams commissioned from Augustus St. Gaudens to commemorate the loss of his wife only a few years earlier. A shrouded sculptural form, bent in solitude and misery, the Adams Memorial (1886-1891) was designed to convey grief in an allegorical sense. Missing is the sense of hope conveyed by Daingerfield.

By 1893, Daingerfield's art had evolved to a mature state. His use of painting to

Illustration 9 – The Mystic Brim, *1893, Oil on canvas, 29 ¼ x 36 inches, 1989.01.038*

The Mystic Brim

*I stood upon the mystic
brim of all Immensity
and now about me
Were forms like seraphim.
Gentle light fell round
the place
I saw go by a company
Moving on eternally,
Their voices mingling in
pure melody.
Dazed I stood and heard
the sound of Hallelujahs
Then this—a soul is saved!
Hallelujah!*[20]

express emotions as well as visions of the spiritual world reflected an awareness of Symbolist developments in European and American art. Symbolism appeared in Europe during the 1880's as a reaction against naturalism and Impressionism in painting. Symbolists painters sought to move beyond the surface of reality, focusing upon an inward vision which reflected their interest in portraying ideas and emotions transcending the world of physical appearances. Odilon Redon, Jean Delville, Fernand Khnopff, Ferdinand Hodler, Jan Toorop and Edvard Munch were among the artists who most directly embodied Symbolist concerns in Europe. Odilon Redon, for example, insisted that his was an intellectual art, filled with mystery and suggestion, which he described for a patron: "My sole aim is to instill in the spectator, by means of unexpected allurements, all the evocations and fascinations of the unknown on the boundaries of thought."[21]

Symbolist influences in American painting, which continued from about 1885 to 1917, have received limited recognition until quite recently. The research of a new generation of art scholars is discovering important American contributions to the development

of international Symbolism. The consideration of Symbolist influences in paintings of the South is even more limited yet offers rich opportunities for greater exploration, as evident in the case of Elliott Daingerfield. The remarkable diversity evident in American Symbolism was brought to public attention when *American Imagination and Symbolist Painting*, an exhibition and accompanying catalogue of the same name, were presented in 1979. Charles Eldredge, writing in the catalogue, acknowledged that at that time, despite growing interest in Symbolist studies, "consensus is still lacking on a definition and dating of the movement."[22] While recognizing that "there was little stylistic coherence to the Symbolist movement" and that Symbolist painters were tied primarily by "attitudes toward their subject, and their mood" he was able to discover a unifying bond: "The Symbolist poets and painters of the late nineteenth century were united in their common reaction against what they saw as the dominant materialist, naturalist and determinist ethos of the epoch. By focusing on the internal, symbolical world rather than the external, empirical one, by resorting to introspection rather than observation, they sought escapes from the tyranny of Fact and the denunciation of Soul which threatened to extinguish the life of the Imagination."[23]

Daingerfield could have first encountered Symbolism through a variety of sources. The first Symbolist poets were based in Paris, yet their influence in music, literature, theater, opera and the visual arts quickly spread throughout the western world.[24] During the 1890s, in publications such as *The Chap-Book*, published in Boston, and *The Bookman, An Illustrated Literary Journal*, published in New York, as well as in popular magazines such as *Harper's* and *Scribner's*, Americans read increasingly about Symbolist writers and painters. In the year he completed *The Mystic Brim*, Daingerfield could have read Aline Gorren's extensive essay on the French Symbolist poets in *Scribner's*, a magazine which later published many of his own essays.[25] In 1897, while traveling in Europe for the first

Illustration 10 – Epiphany, 1902-1905, Mural, In the Lady Chapel of St. Mary the Virgin, New York City, New York.

time, he probably discovered many Symbolist paintings well before they became widely known in the United States.

In 1893, Daingerfield also would have recognized that the growing importance of the American mural offered an ideal medium to merge his Symbolist and religious concerns in a manner ideally suited to reaching, and inspiring, audiences. The opening of the 1893 World's Columbian Exposition in Chicago marked an important moment in the evolution of the American mural tradition. Many American artists found the mural to be an ideal forum for a didactic, morally uplifting form of public art. Increasingly, as Richard Murray has suggested, "in the artists' and architects' minds, and in that of the public… murals became a necessary ingredient for decorative schemes in large and small buildings alike. From the exposition, too, arose a new civic image, a need to allegorize or place in a historical context modern events, technology, and ideas."[26] America's growing world stature and its related wealth, while morally troubling to many artists, especially one who had survived the lasting realities of the Civil War in the South, offered abundant opportunities to reach audiences with enlightened civic lessons. With the opening of the new Library of Congress in 1897, described as "our national monument of art" by contemporary critic Royal Cortissoz, the public stature of the mural painter had achieved a level previously unknown to artists in this country.[27]

The creation of murals, especially murals expanding the themes of his religious paintings, offered significant opportunities for Daingerfield. In 1896, his popular painting, *Madonna and Child*, was purchased by Haley Fiske, President of the Metropolitan Life Insurance Company. Six years later, in 1902, Fiske commissioned Daingerfield to paint murals for the chapel at St. Mary the Virgin in New York City. "It was," notes Robert Hobbs, "the commission of the decade, and Elliott Daingerfield suddenly the man of the moment, inspired a large audience of admirers."[28] He began the first of the two murals, *The Epiphany*, depicting the Adoration of the Magi, in 1902 and completed it in 1905 (*illustration 10*). The second mural, *The Magnificat*, showing the Virgin following the Annunciation, was completed in the following year. The Morris Museum now owns a large number of Daingerfield's original sketches for the figures included in the mural, (*illustrations 11*). In these works Daingerfield's power as a draftsman, his compositional skills and his abilities as a colorist show him to be one of the leading academic artists of his time.

A series of Symbolist and Tonalist landscapes, painted from 1895 to 1915, reflect the continuing influence of Inness and Ryder upon Daingerfield's vision of the American landscape. They also suggest that Daingerfield's approach to the landscape in these years, especially prior to 1910, may have incorporated uniquely Southern attitudes which have been little recognized in the larger field of American landscape studies. In his description of the importance of the Symbolist landscape in the South, Bruce Chambers suggests that, despite the obvious appeal of the Impressionist palette, Southern artists were more commonly

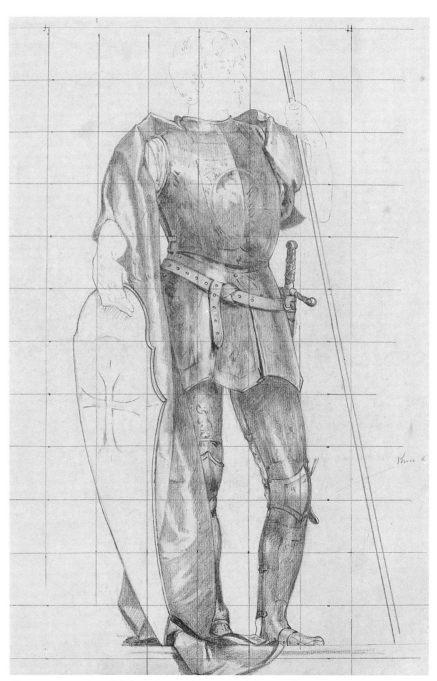

Illustration 11 – Archangel Michael - Armor and Drapery Study for Magnificat, 1902-1906
Graphite on paper, 19⅝ x 15¼ inches, 1993.C0925

involved "with interpreting the world that lay behind appearances than they were with the transient effects of surface." He concludes that the Symbolist approach to the landscape of the South offered an alternative path which meshed with distinctive regional attitudes: "In part, this reflected the South's general distrust of 'foreign' styles, but there was also a pride in the

principle that the South was somehow removed from the mundane, materialistic concerns of the North and was a place holier and more sacrosanct in its associations."[29]

Mysterious Night, exhibited in 1895, depicts a moonlit scene in the Carolinas which illustrates this Southern sensibility (*illustration 12*). The massive and gnarled trunk of a mature tree dominates the foreground, while dark, cloudlike branches diffuse the light of the moon. Reflected moonlight marks the roof of a barn and a row of fence posts in the middle distance, with the enclosed farmyard bathed in a pool of light. The moon may be emerging from the branches or, more pointedly, it may soon be consumed by the shadowy profile of this ancient tree, itself, no doubt, a silent witness to countless mysterious passages. The scene is filled with the possibilities of a Southern gothic encounter, leaving the viewer to speculate upon the nature of the place and this evening.

Illustration 12 – Mysterious Night, 1895, Watercolor on board, 30½ x 21½ inches, 1989.01.043

It is the mood, the artist's response to a specific moment, in *Mysterious Night* that is more important than a literal depiction of a specific locale. Informed by Inness's personal approach to the landscape and Ryder's unique vision, which often incorporated moonlit imagery and shadowy forms, Daingerfield painted his subjective response to a particular place and time. In recent decades, scholars have applied the term Tonalism (or Quietism) to describe such a subjective, personalized style of landscape painting. His interest in this subject and this approach to painting may have been intensified by an awareness of the importance of moonlit imagery in Southern literature and mythology. His discovery of the writings of Algernon Blackwood during this same period, a writer known for his interest in psychic phenomenon and a pantheist's approach to the natural world, certainly contributed to the mood of this work.[30]

Grandfather Mountain, a watercolor painted in 1910 (*illustration 13*), reflects a response to the clouds and atmospheric conditions evident at a favorite site in the mountains near his North Carolina studio. Once again, however, he uses a familiarity with a

Illustration 13 – Grandfather Mountain, N.C., *1910, Watercolor on paper, 9 x 12¼ inches, 1989.01.044*

specific site to create an image which transcends the particular to suggest more universal concerns. In this and a related watercolor of Grandfather Mountain (*illustration 14*) painted in the same period, clouds and mist serve to diffuse light and to obscure the mass of the mountains. The effect is similar to that employed in the evening scene, *Mysterious Night*. These atmospheric renderings demonstrate his skills as a watercolorist and evoke the mood of traditional Chinese paintings of mountain vistas. This intimate work, measuring only 9 x 12 inches, also relates to his earliest aesthetic responses to the overwhelming scale and atmosphere he discovered at the Grand Canyon during his 1910 visit.

Illustration 14 – Grandfather Mountain, N.C., 1910-1920, Watercolor on paper, 9¼ x 13¼ inches
1993.C0176

A later painting, *Sunset Glory* (c. 1915), shows how these concerns continued beyond the year 1910, even after his visits to the Grand Canyon and the West. Once again, a tree dominates the foreground, framing the viewer's perspective and serving as a foil to the brilliance of the colorful North Carolina sky in the distance (*illustration 15*). A focus on the spectacle of the sunset may suggest a response to the dramatic Western sunsets he had seen by this date, or it may relate to earlier American landscapes, including the paintings of Frederic Edwin Church. The mood and pantheistic sensitivity to the presence of a quieter, but equally powerful, divine presence tie this work to a distinct moment in the evolution of the American landscape tradition. Paintings such as this, in the opinion of Diana Sweet, link Daingerfield to the "Tonalist aesthetic of poetic conception based on memory, intimate personal style, and enriched colors, which represent a mood rather than a specific locale."[31]

Daingerfield summarized his attitude toward the landscape in "Nature Versus Art," published in *Scribner's* in 1911: "The oft-repeated phrase, 'Paint from Nature,' is a good one if properly understood: Paint from – in the sense of away – not by her, lest she has her way with you and not you with her. My meaning is made clear by quoting from one of our very distinguished artists – 'What we want is less nature and more art.'"[32] *Carolina Sunlight*

A view from Westglow, Daingerfield's North Carolina home. Here, the mood and atmosphere of familiar surroundings dictated the direction of his inspiration rather than the specifics of the tangible world.

Illustration 15 – Sunset Glory, c. 1915, Oil on canvas, 27½ x 33¼ inches, 1990.014

Illustration 16 – Carolina Sunlight, c. 1915, Oil on canvas, 24 x 28¼ inches, 1989.01.045

(*illustration 16*) completed in the same period as *Sunset Glory*, offers a model of his concept of painting "from Nature." Rick Stewart refers to *Carolina Sunlight* as a prime example of the artist's transcendence of traditional attitudes toward the landscape. "The view of nature in 'Carolina Sunlight' begins as an evocation of the artist's own childhood in North Carolina but passes quickly to a higher 'vision of order,' to borrow a phrase from Richard Weaver…" In Weaver's words, nature becomes "a refuge of sentiments and values," particularly suited to the South, with a base of traditional Christian beliefs and unlimited possibilities for forging new connections to the culture of the modern age. Daingerfield, Stewart believes, recognized these opportunities: "The 'vision of order' conveyed in works like *Carolina Sunlight* is an attempt to reconcile what Weaver termed 'the permanent moral reality' of the Southern landscape with the larger goals of the creative imagination."[33]

By 1910, Daingerfield's abilities as a painter of landscapes, religious subjects, murals and introspective, Symbolist imagery, had earned him critical respect and public recognition. While maintaining studios in New York and Blowing Rock, he taught and began to write about art and artists. In 1902, he was elected to associate membership in the National Academy of Design. The following year, he was elected to membership in the Society of American Painters. By 1906, he achieved his goal of full membership in the National Academy of Design, completing a cycle that was initiated in 1880, the year he exhibited one of his first New York paintings at the Academy. In 1910, after reaching a notable point in his professional career, Daingerfield was invited to accompany a group of artists in an expedition to the American West, a region that he had never visited. It proved to be a providential opportunity.

DAINGERFIELD AND VISIONS OF THE GRAND CANYON

Daingerfield was one of five American artists who gathered in Chicago on the evening of November 5, 1910, for a private dinner hosted at the Union League Club. Later that evening the artists and members of their party boarded a private rail car provided by the Atchison, Topeka and Santa Fe Railway. The artists on board, including Thomas Moran, Frederick Ballard, Edward Potthast and DeWitt Parshall, were bound for Arizona, commissioned by the railroad to capture on canvas the spirit of the Grand Canyon. For Daingerfield, travelling west of Chicago for the first time, the trip would have a profound impact upon his art, far transcending the original purpose of the journey. The western venture would also initiate his final, and most notable, period of Symbolist painting in the years prior to America's involvement in the World War.

Three days after leaving Chicago the party arrived at the Grand Canyon railhead. They were transported to the El Tovar Hotel and then immediately on to Hopi Point to experience a viewing of the canyon at sunset. They were accompanied by a writer, Nina Spalding Stevens, who described their journey and first impressions of the canyon in the February, 1911 issue of *Fine Arts Journal*: "The artists were led to the rim with their eyes closed, that the vision might burst upon them for the first time in its entirety. All was still with the silence of infinity… It was as though the earth had opened before them and heaven was spread at their feet."[34]

They watched, in silence, as the light began to evaporate and as "the distant towers and domes changed from pink to blue" leaving only the pinnacles illuminated. Consistent with nineteenth century accounts of the sublime, describing man's interaction with a Divine Creator through the evidence of an abundant and awesome natural paradise, their experience was more than visual: "The awful depth became mysterious and terrifying and no sound was heard save the rushing of the wind through the pines and a far away murmur of the mighty rapids of the Colorado a mile below." At the conclusion of this spectacle they returned to the El Tovar: "No word was spoken on the homeward drive."[35]

The Grand Canyon had inspired a wide range of visitors before the arrival of this small band of artists. John Muir wrote: "Nature has a few big places beyond man's power to spoil—the ocean, the two icy ends of the globe, and the Grand Canyon of Arizona."[36] Speaking at the Canyon in 1903, Theodore Roosevelt proclaimed it "the one great sight which every American should see" and called for its continuing preservation: "The Grand Canyon of Arizona fills me with awe. It is beyond comparison... Let this great wonder of nature remain as it now is. Do nothing to mar its grandeur, sublimity and loveliness."[37] As the nineteenth century gave way to the progressive march of the twentieth century, anti-modernist sentiments became increasingly evident. The appearance of automobiles, modern cities filled with skyscrapers and the accompanying disruption of a rural society caused many to look longingly to the past. Roosevelt recognized the need for unspoiled beauty and natural wonders such as the Grand Canyon to balance the rapid changes overtaking American society. Here, he believed, the twentieth century might confront the timeless realities of nature as well as the evidence of creative forces greater than the hand of man.

If any American painter deserved to be considered the original master of the Grand Canyon that artist was surely Thomas Moran. Even though his approach to the American landscape reflected a different philosophy and generational attitude, Daingerfield was fortunate to accompany him on this journey and to see the canyon through the eyes of an artist who served as a direct tie to the late traditions of the Hudson River School. Moran's paintings of the Grand Canyon of the Yellowstone had inspired Eastern audiences and contributed to the designation of Yellowstone as the first national park in 1872. He had first visited and painted this region when he accompanied John Wesley Powell and his surveying party on its exploration of the Grand Canyon of the Colorado in 1873. Almost

twenty years later, in 1892, the Santa Fe Railway invited Moran to return to paint the canyon. With expenses paid by the railroad, it asked only for the rights to use one of his Canyon paintings in its advertising campaign.

Because of its remote location, the Grand Canyon remained a mysterious and relatively inaccessible destination until the turn of the century. To visit the Canyon in 1892 Moran had traveled by stagecoach from Flagstaff, an arduous journey. During the late 1890s, while it worked to bring a rail line to the edge of the canyon, the Santa Fe Railway looked for ways to promote the splendors of the Canyon as well as other destinations along its lines in the Southwest. One of its most successful campaigns featured the distribution of thousands of lithographs of Moran's painting, some in gilt frames, to schools, offices, hotels and individuals throughout the country. When the first Santa Fe engine arrived at the south rim of the canyon on September 18, 1901, it was a momentous occasion. By 1905, with the completion of the El Tovar Hotel and final plans for tourist accommodations by Fred Harvey, the stage was set for the real beginning of the tourist trade at the Grand Canyon.[38]

Moran returned to the canyon in the summer of 1901, in the company of George Inness, Jr. and George McCord, just before the rail line was completed. Soon after this visit, he published an article devoted to American art and the scenery of the West. His goal was "to call the attention of American landscape painters to the unlimited field for the exercise of their talents to be found in this enchanting southwestern country." The Arizona territory merited particular attention: "This Grand Canyon of Arizona, and all the country surrounding it, offers a new and comparatively untrodden field for pictorial interpretation, and only awaits the men of original thoughts and ideas to prove to their countrymen that we possess a land of beauty and grandeur with which no other can compare." He concluded by appealing to a wide range of American painters: "The pastoral painter, the painter of picturesque genre, the imaginative and dramatic landscapist are here offered all that can delight the eye or stir the imagination and emotions!"[39]

Such a clarion call, issued in eloquent terms by an old master of the American landscape, would have been most appealing to an artist of Daingerfield's inclinations. Moran viewed the 1910 pilgrimage as the fulfillment of his desires and an answer to his challenge to the painters of the Eastern landscape. In her account of the journey, Nina Spalding remembered that "during these ten days the Canyon displaying all of her emotions, glided from summer into the depths of winter. Storms came and filled the chasm with softest clouds… now veiling and now unclosing visions of infinite beauty." The arrival of the group was summarized in auspicious terms: "Never before had so large a group of serious artists made such a pilgrimage to the far west with the avowed intention of studying a given point of their own country, and thus will this visit to the Canyon become historical."[40]

On his first morning at the Canyon, Daingerfield, like the others in his party, arose at dawn to make observations and notes. His response to the location was memorable: "Mr. Daingerfield was sometimes silent and, sometimes colorful adjectives came tumbling from his lips in a passion of appreciation. Words which in his moments of ecstasy came nearer to describing the emotions of the Canyon than the most finished efforts of authors and poets." What is most telling, when considering the visionary paintings he would soon complete, is the following observation by one of his contemporaries: "What mysterious forms of beauty, invisible to the rest, peopled the Canyon for him! For Nature is to Daingerfield an embodied spirit."[41]

Daingerfield's first paintings of the Canyon focused on his response to the intensive light, colors and atmospheric conditions he encountered on his initial visit. In a small oil sketch, *Grand Canyon #2*, two trees are placed in the foreground, as the focal point, with the canyon in the distance suggesting a seemingly infinite space (*illustration 17*). The use of trees as central compositional devices had become a well established tradition in his paintings of North Carolina by this time. A subject as seemingly simple as these trees, however, had enormous implications for Daingerfield, as he explained: "To Mr. Daingerfield the pres-

Illustration 17 – Grand Canyon #2, c. 1911-1913, Oil on board, 10 x 8 inches, 1993.C0179

ence of a tree against a sky is as real and vital in its message bearing quality as is a mother with her child. It is the thing that is pervaded with mystery, and that mystery is the presence of God in all His works."[42] If Daingerfield's inclinations toward a pantheistic point of view were ever to find the perfect subject it would be here, at the Grand Canyon.

Illustration 18 – The Lifting Veil, 1913, Oil on canvas, 32 x 48 inches, Courtesy of the Santa Fe Railway, Schaumburg, Illinois

Following this first visit to Arizona and the West, Daingerfield produced a diverse range of paintings devoted to the Grand Canyon and themes suggested by his experiences there. Robert Hobbs, the curator of the Daingerfield retrospective exhibition presented in 1971, found that the artist first saw the Canyon "in a spectacular and full blown form. He spotted the same colors he had known and painted in North Carolina, but the Colorado [sic] sun intensified them and made them more luminous."[43]   Two of his paintings, *The Divine Abyss* (1911) and *The Lifting Veil, Grand Canyon* (1913), entered and still remain in the collection of the Santa Fe Railway. *The Lifting Veil* (*illustration 18*) was recently shown in Santa Fe as part of an exhibition devoted to the art and artists associated with the pioneering era of the Santa Fe Railroad.[44]   In this work, the grandeur of the canyon is amplified by atmospheric effects, subtle coloration and light patterns which depict the realities of the changing environment. The use of cloud patterns and diffused light, while unique in application, had been explored in his earlier paintings of the North Carolina mountains, including works such as *Grandfather Mountain*.

Illustration 19 – The Lone Cypress, c. 1913-1915, Oil on canvas, 30¼ x 36¼ inches, 1993.C 0695

Daingerfield's first expedition to the West made a deep and lasting impression. So much so that he made a second journey in 1913, this time accompanied by his family. The journey included a stay in Carmel, California, and a return to the Grand Canyon. During this period he probably received the inspiration for *The Lone Cypress,* a work which includes the continuing motif of the tree as rugged survivor, in this instance one twisted in response to the rigors of wind and sea (*illustration 19*). The form of the cypress dominates the composition, contrasting with the expressive colors of the sky and background, and towering over the humans who are reduced to a small supporting role in the distance. The most successful paintings produced from 1913 to 1915 are characterized by a Symbolist orientation and a broader visionary sweep than many of the earlier works, including those produced for the railroad (which had specific promotional and publicity requirements asso-

ciated with the commission). In his autobiographical sketch, Daingerfield explained his methodology: " When he goes to the Grand Canyon he makes his studies in the simple, student like way that he believes right and proper for all students to do, and when he paints his picture it has some of the great principle which he asks us to see."[45]

That "great principle" was evident in one of his most ambitious paintings. *The Genius of the Canyon,* painted in 1913, depicts a female nude, draped along the rocks in the foreground, head lowered in sleep or contemplation, long hair flowing toward the emptiness of the canyon (*illustration 20*). In the distance a domed architectural fantasy, illuminated by an ethereal glow, emerges from the distant rock forms. In this painting, Daingerfield brought to life the "distant towers and domes" alluded to by visitors to the canyon. He described, in the third person voice adapted for his autobiography, how this

Illustration 20 – The Genius of the Canyon, *1913, Oil on canvas, 36 x 48½ inches, 1989.01.039*

Detail of the city – The Genius of the Canyon

painting responded to the site: "While he uses sufficient of the Canyon form to make us sure of what we see, he tells us, for instance, of the silence of the Canyon. That he manifests and expresses by the use of a great figure." He concludes by describing the other related Symbolist compositions in this series: "Or again, he will tell you of the vast age and somnolence of this great freak of nature, and we find carved into the rocks titan figures of vast proportions sleeping in the midst of the silence; or if he calls a storm into being, he symbolizes the Storm Spirit."[46]

As he did when painting the *Mystic Brim*, Daingerfield planned this work to be accompanied by a poem which added another dimension to the experience of viewing the completed work. Later, he would be referred to as the "genius of the canyon" because of the fame of these works:

> *Strip From the Earth Her Crust,*
> *And See Revealed the Carven Glory of the Inner World,*
> *Templed, – Domed, – Silent: –*
> *The While the Genius of the Canyon Broods*
> *Nor Counts the Ages of Mankind*
> *A Thought Amid the Everlasting Calm.*[47]

Illustration 21 – The Sleepers, 1914, *Oil on canvas mounted on board, 36 x 48⅛ inches, 1993.C0814*

One year later, still exploring his vision of the merging of allegorical figures with the mysteries of the canyon, he completed *The Sleepers (illustration 21)*. Here, instead of one figure, he presents a group of figures, male and female, draped in repose along the rim of the canyon. The male forms, all suggestive of the revived appreciation of Michelangelo's figures evident in these years, reside in the shadows facing the canyon with bright light glowing in the distance. Elsewhere he had alluded to this work, "carved into the rocks titan figures of vast proportions sleeping in the midst of the silence." One of the studies for this painting shows his reliance upon his academic drawing skills *(illustration 22)* and suggests the progressive stages he would have followed to reach the final figurative arrangement of *The Sleepers*. The half nude female form, reposing horizontally and bathed in subtle light along the front of the picture plane, reflects the use of a similar female figure in *The Genius of the Canyon*. A poem was created for this work as well:

> *Age on age the Sleepers rest,*
> *To see in dreams the Canyon's splendor rise*
> *Height on height, from river bed to golden crest.*
> *Gods are they! – as you and I –*
> *Who see in spirit what the eyes deny.*[48]

A third and related painting of the Grand Canyon, *The Spirit of the Storm*, *(illustration 23)* is now a part of the American art collection at Reynolda House. This painting, also referred to in the excerpt from Daingerfield's autobiographical sketch, is dated about 1912, but was probably painted in this 1913-1915 period. This work also features a half-draped, allegorical female figure who stands, rather than reclines, prominently in the foreground. Her hair blowing actively in the wind, back to the viewer as she faces the canyon with her right arm and hand raised toward it, we see in the distance a cloudy and indistinct view of the Grand Canyon. This atmospheric perspective relates to a similar view in *The Lifting Veil* and, once again, seems to carry the viewer back to his watercolor

Grandfather Mountain. In this work as well, light, color and dramatic atmosphere contribute to the tone, the mood of the work. The painting seems to illustrate Nina Spalding's earlier quoted observation that during their 1910 visit to the canyon storms "came and filled the chasm with softest clouds…now veiling and now unclosing visions of infinite beauty." No accompanying poem is known to exist for this painting.[49]

With these original and memorable paintings, Daingerfield recorded his distinctive response to the spirit and energies of the Canyon. They serve as documents of what he saw and felt there, capturing his sense of what D.H. Lawrence called the "spirit of place." As an artist who maintained direct ties to the region of his birth, deriving inspiration and sustenance from the soil and spirit of the South, he had a refined sensitivity to the particular nuance of place. In time, as he came to know the Canyon, and to trust his deeper responses to the remarkable presence of this location, his paintings grew in vision and power. They also reflected themes which were consistent with international Symbolism.

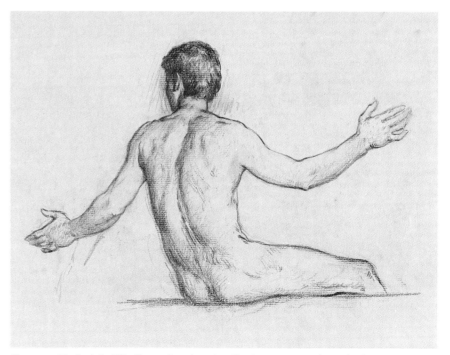

Illustration 22 – Study for "The Sleepers," c. 1913-1914, Graphite on paper, 12⅛ x 16¼ inches, 1993.C0927

Illustration 23 – Spirit of the Storm, 1912, Oil on canvas, 36 x 48 ⅜ inches, Courtesy of Reynolda House, Museum of American Art, Winston-Salem, North Carolina

The inclusion of Symbolist painters at the Armory Show of 1913, while minimized in later histories, brought original works by leading European artists to the attention of the New York art world. Odilon Redon, who had remained relatively unknown to American audiences until this exhibition, had the largest one person representation in the Armory Show, with a total of 75 prints and paintings displayed.[50] The inclusion of Symbolists in this influential exhibition, and the resulting impact on the New York art world, would have reinforced Daingerfield's appreciation of these artists and encouraged even bolder personal experiments and explorations.

Presentations of sleeping and dreamlike states were common in Symbolist painting. While sleeping, particularly when dreaming, the mind was freed from constraints and open to deeper messages from the unconscious. The portrayal of sleeping figures suggested not just a mind at rest, it implied a level of unseen activity occupying the mind and senses of the subject. By the end of the nineteenth century there was growing interest in understanding dream states and in the interpretation of dreams. In the early twentieth century Freud's theories became widely known and contributed to an even greater interest in the relationship between the unconscious mind and the creative process. Also common was a related fascination with synaesthesia, explained as the appeal to multiple senses, ranging from music to poetry and other art forms, combined in ways to suggest expanded visual or aural experiences. Certain colors might be used, for example, to suggest specific moods or harmonies.[51]

What does this suggest about Daingerfield's canyon figures? Are the dreams of *The Sleepers* explained in his poem? The sleeping giants, bent in repose, may indeed "see in dreams the Canyon's splendor rise" and also "see in spirit what the eyes deny." Perhaps they embody the visions of Daingerfield who seems to have moved far beyond his colleagues in his perceptions of the realities of the Canyon. In *The Genius of the Canyon* a solitary, allegorical figure of great elegance is, we learn from his poem, seeing, with eyes closed, what rests beneath the surface of the Canyon. The "inner world" contains an architectural fantasy, "templed, domed, silent," which suggests perhaps the floating, ephemeral qualities of classic Venetian architecture. Throughout the nineteenth century, the depiction of vision-

ary architectural forms was a distinctive interest for a small number of American painters. However, the inclusion of the dreamer or individual responsible for the image was decidedly less common.

The allegorical paintings of Thomas Cole often incorporated architectural forms. In *The Course Of Empire*, completed in 1836, he painted a series of architectural environments which mirrored the patterns of empire from early, bucolic states to late, crumbling architectural ruins. In Cole's painting of 1840, *The Voyage of Life, Youth*, a domed, heavenly temple appears as a vision in a brilliant flood of celestial light. In *The Architect's Dream* Cole actually depicts the dreamer, a reclining architect, who looks over a panorama of classical and gothic architectural forms. Thomas Moran, Daingerfield's early guide to the mysteries of the canyon, was also well known for his ethereal images of Venice as was J.M.W. Turner. A city of classical structures, floating over and reflected in the waters, including those of the canals, Venice was a natural attraction for artists of such a taste. Daingerfield's fantasy in the *Genius of the Canyon* may suggest these Venetian forms. After 1924, Daingerfield himself painted a series of Venetian scenes indicating that this may have been an early manifestation of a continuing interest. The classical form shown in *The Sleepers* seems more grounded, perhaps closer to an American acropolis or a gesture to the earlier temples of Cole. Or, possibly, this was an allusion to Albert Pinkham Ryder's influential *Temple of the Mind*, painted circa 1885, which was, in Symbolist fashion, a response to a poem written by Edgar Allen Poe, *The Haunted Palace*.[52]

As Daingerfield's poems indicate, the figures in *The Genius of the Canyon* and *The Sleepers* are active, not passive. They "see revealed" and "see in dreams" what others do not, or will not, perceive. Reflecting the principles of synaesthesia, the figures also may be listening, underscoring the importance of both sound and silence. Even with no human presence, the natural environment of the canyon is filled with sounds and possible suggestions of harmonies beyond those of the earthly realm. Notably, when Daingerfield and his companions first viewed the Grand Canyon at sunset, sound was a profound part of the experience, as Nina Spalding remembered: "The awful depth became mysterious and terrifying and no sound was heard save the rushing of the wind through the pines and a far away murmur of the mighty rapids of the Colorado a mile below." For those who visit the Canyon, especially for those venture to its lower depths, it is common to look and to listen in a state of heightened awareness of the natural order, and to consider the temporal world and the sources of this geological wonder. Daingerfield's poem points to such greater harmonies: "The While the Genius of the Canyon Broods/ Nor Counts the Ages of Mankind/ A Thought Amid the Everlasting Calm."

DAINGERFIELD, SYMBOLISM AND THE SOUTHERN AESTHETIC

After 1915, the focus of Daingerfield's aesthetic vision began to move away from the Grand Canyon and, equally, away from the Symbolist concerns which had occupied him for over two decades. Demonstrating his permanent ties to the soil and the mountains of the South, he constructed a new studio, Westglow, which was completed in 1916 (*illustration 24*). Soon after painting classical temples in the spirit of Cole and Moran in his Grand Canyon vistas he was able to return to build a real temple on a hill overlooking the mountains of North Carolina. The dream, in this case, became a reality. Incorporating the traditions of the Greek Revival style, the design of Westglow referred not only to the classical past but also to the now distant and increasingly mythic spirit of the antebellum South. Perhaps the house he watched Union forces burn in the childhood years of the Civil War was finally replaced, in spirit and in reality. He described his time in Blowing Rock during these years as an idyllic experience: "And so in his mountain home in the Blue Ridge mountains of North Carolina, where he spends his summers in an almost primeval environment, he is watching the majesty of the storm, the splendor of the sunset, the gray swirl of fog clouds, and the flowing change of season upon season ...."[53]

In the mountains of North Carolina he found familiar surroundings, inspiration and, significantly, refuge from the turmoil of a changing American cultural environment. Here, he wrote, he constantly sought a "higher expression," refusing to descend to "the use of the petty, of the common place ...." In contrast, he described the cloistered nature of his New York lifestyle: "He is working to-day in his prime in the environment of New York, but in a studio which is shut away, where he objects to anything intruding that is not of his art, that is not of a reverential character – and there in this privacy he exploits no painter's tricks nor skillful gesticulations, but in the smallest thing teaches of a beauty which only they may see who view it with the eyes of the spirit."[54]

Although New York's art world had nurtured Daingerfield's career and his vision

Westglow, completed in 1916, reflected the classical past and the antebellum South of Daingerfield's youth.

Illustration 24 —Westglow, c. 1917, Oil on board, 12 x 16 inches, 1993.CXX08

since 1880, he began to withdraw from a radically changing urban milieu which bore little resemblance to the city he first encountered. In the years from 1908 to 1917, when his focus shifted from religious murals to the Grand Canyon projects, the contemporary art world changed around him. Robert Henri and the Eight, the so-called Ash Can School, exhibited their paintings of realistic urban scenes. Alfred Stieglitz introduced many Americans to modern art at his 291 gallery. A new generation of artists and writers motivated by modernism, iconoclasm and a rejection of past traditions ushered in a new era. The very foundations of art appeared shattered as cubism then abstraction reflected radically new ways of seeing. As an intelligent and perceptive veteran of the New York art scene, Daingerfield surely realized that he had become a member of that most dreaded group which he had rejected in his own youth, the older generation.

In 1916, as Daingerfield finished his Greek Revival studio in Blowing Rock, and worked on paintings titled *Return from the Farm* and *The Red Sofa Cushion*, America's modernists exhibited a wide range of vital new works at "The Forum Exhibition of Modern American Painters." Presented at the Anderson Galleries, this significant exhibition featured 193 paintings by seventeen artists including Thomas Hart Benton, Arthur Dove, Marsden Hartley, John Marin, Man Ray, Morgan Russell, Charles Sheeler and Abraham Walkowitz.[55] The new generation was well represented in this show which may have served as one of the objects of Daingerfield's growing anti-modernist sentiment. In "George Inness," an article he published in *The Century Magazine* in 1917, Daingerfield praised the purity and depth of his mentor's vision and took the opportunity to comment on the passing scene: "During his working days there were as many isms abroad as there are to-day, but he would have none of them, realizing keenly, as most thoughtful men do, that their lure is rather to the man who has no power of thought, of invention, within himself; that it is not, and, in its own nature, cannot be born of sincerity."[56]

Daingerfield was far from alone in calling for an art of sincerity, originality and purity of vision. His colleague Kenyon Cox wrote *The Classic Point of View* in 1911 to defend the principles of his generation from the criticisms of modernists. In words and tone similar to Daingerfield's he explained their traditionalists' perspective: "The Classic Spirit is the disinterested search for perfection; it is the love of clearness and reasonableness and self-control; it is, above all, the love of permanence and continuity.....And it loves to steep itself in tradition."[57] The defense of tradition, of the ways of the past, of the established order, had become a major concern at the turn of the century. When necessary, new traditions were invented and then quickly defended as ancient truths. "The idea of instant traditions seemed neither an oxymoron nor absurd," explains Michael Kammen in his recent study of this period. "A hunger for tradition developed in Victorian America."[58] In the South, despite the efforts of Henry Grady and proponents of a "New South," traditions persisted and multiplied at the turn of the century, as indicated by the strength of the Confederate revival and the explosion of interest in genealogy.[59]

Daingerfield may have felt that he was traveling from one century to the next as he shuttled between Blowing Rock and New York City, then recognized internationally as the most modern city in the world. After the World War, he continuing to paint, to write and to study the course of American art in these two radically different environments. In 1924, he was able to return to Europe and to spend time in Venice. Perhaps amplified by the rigors of the European journey, he suffered a serious physical breakdown in 1925 which severely limited his ability to paint. However, until the time of his death, at his studio in New York, in 1932, Daingerfield continued to paint and to explore Venetian views which may, in many different ways, have been a continuation of the architectural visions he had initiated in his paintings of the Grand Canyon (*illustration 25*).

A memorial exhibition, featuring over fifty of his paintings, was held at Grand Central Galleries in New York on April 3-21, 1934. Throughout his career, Daingerfield and his art never fit neatly into simple categories or satisfied those who look for simplistic interpretations of art and its "meaning." Even in 1971, when the Mint Museum of Art presented the only retrospective exhibition of Daingerfield's art, the curator, Robert Hobbs, found that the artist "defies classification." The range of his work contributed to this dilemma: "At times he varies from being an 'American Millet' to having affinities with the Pre-Raphaelites. Adjectives as Western, Ryderesque, or American Decorative Impressionist apply only to certain periods of his painting. . . ." Even looking to the artists and critics of the time did not resolve the issue for Hobbs: "His contemporaries referred to him as a tonalistic, or colorist, or called him an intimate painter. But labels such as these do not describe the complete man."[60] Conspicuously missing from this list is the term Symbolist. Because American art historians would not begin to seriously reconsider the importance of Symbolism in the art of this country until the end of the 1970s, his omission is not surprising.

Daingerfield's vision of America, and of the South, in the years from 1893 to 1917 may have been distinctive but it was far from an isolated, singular perspective. It was part of a larger fabric, that of the Symbolist aesthetic which was evident in Europe and America from about 1885 until 1917. After 1917 the spirit and interests of the nation changed. With the World War, and America's entrance into that conflagration, there was a fundamental shift in the mood of the country. The end of the American Renaissance had arrived along with the end of the Symbolist era. The beginning of the "Jazz Age," the "Roaring Twenties," was not far off. Daingerfield's sensitivities were, without doubt, far removed from the directions of the 1920s. His was a spirit deeply connected to an older order, what Kenyon Cox had called the "Classic Point of View." And, as Rick Stewart discovered, Daingerfield's art remained deeply connected to the unique attitudes of the South: "To him, the artist did not just paint nature but actually became nature in his work. Like so many Southern landscape artists of the period, he had an individual view that began with a highly developed sense of place, including the belief that the artist had to draw his material

Illustration 25 – A Dream of Venice, c. 1924, Oil on canvas, 30 x 36 inches

from his native area in order to achieve spiritual and artistic regeneration."[61] To properly understand Elliott Daingerfield's life and work in this period he must be considered not just as an American Symbolist but also as a Symbolist working in the South.

As a Symbolist working in the South, Daingerfield's art and philosophies were tied not just to the era of the "New South" but to the antebellum South and the histories of the Romantic movement in the South. His sources incorporated the art, literature, music, myths, history and traditions of the American South. If Symbolism included a dark, brooding, introspective dimension, removed from the capitalistic optimism evident at the turn of the century, then the South was a natural source of inspiration for a Symbolist artist. Here, as Michael Kammen observes, after the Civil War a series of "unresolved tensions" arose from a ground of "oppositional possibilities" including "the imperative of remembering versus the comforting inconvenience of amnesia; reconciliation versus intransigence; the virtues of a New South versus the romance of a Lost Cause; and conflicting perceptions of patriotism versus treason."[62] Ruin, the lingering pains of slavery and ruminations on the past fused to form a rich and fertile soil in which to plant Symbolist roots.

During the 1920s and 1930s, an important new generation of Southern writers and artists used these and related Southern themes to create a remarkable body of distinctive literature and art, what has been called the Southern Renaissance. Daingerfield was, in important ways, a forerunner of this generation, particularly in his ability to transcend the details of place and his own family history to aspire to universal truths and timeless images. For Daingerfield, connections to place were not literal bonds nor should they be viewed as such. Because of his roots in the South, which he nurtured and maintained until his death, he was able to bring a unique perspective and sensitivity to other landscapes, including that of the Grand Canyon.

At the Grand Canyon, in one of the most distant and remote corners of the West, a responsive chord was struck for Daingerfield. Here, because of his openness to the spirit of place, his attunement to the natural environment, he was able to achieve great moments of creativity and insight. Interestingly, there are few, if any, works existing to suggest that

Daingerfield ever painted or responded to the environment of New York City, even though he spent much of his life there. Daingerfield, it seems, had a transcendental sense of place and time. Though rooted in specific locales, especially in Blowing Rock and at the Grand Canyon, he sought, through place and the spirit of these specific locations, a universal truth. His was not, by any means, a provincial or regional view. It was the highest form of seeing that he pursued while painting in these often spectacular geographic retreats. His goals and his vision transcended boundaries.

The thoughtful and perceptive Elliott Daingerfield concisely expressed his conviction about the place of art in the flow of history, offering what may be the best summation of the accomplishments of this artist whose life spanned the era from the Civil War to the early years of the Great Depression: "A great value in a work of art is that we may read the man in his work, nay: more—we may read the man and his time, and art which is immortal renders a people immortal."[63]

– J. RICHARD GRUBER

FOOTNOTES

1. Daingerfield quoted in Robert Hobbs, *Elliott Daingerfield Retrospective Exhibition*, Charlotte, North Carolina: The Mint Museum of Art, 1971, p. 40. This definition of art was included in his lecture to the Girls High School in Louisville, Kentucky in 1895 and reprinted in the *Louisville Courier Journal* on April 19, 1895.
2. Elliott Daingerfield, "Sketch of his Life—written by Elliott Daingerfield—in response to a request," unpublished and undated manuscript, Elliott Daingerfield estate files, Center for the Study of Southern Painting, p. 2.
3. Ibid., p. 1.
4. Richard N. Murray, "Painting and Sculpture," in *The American Renaissance, 1876-1917*, New York: The Brooklyn Museum, 1979, pp. 154-155. For additional information on the academic tradition see: Lois Marie Fink and Joshua C. Taylor, *Academy, The Academic Tradition in American Art*, Washington: Smithsonian Institution Press, 1975.

5. Henry Adams quoted in Michael Kammen, *Mystic Chords of Memory, The Transformation of Tradition in American Culture*, New York: Vintage Books, 1993, p. 93.
6. Murray, "Painting and Sculpture," p. 155.
7. Hobbs, *Elliott Daingerfield*, pp. 12-14.
8. Doreen Bolger Burke and Catherine Hoover Voorsanger, "The Hudson River School in Eclipse," in *American Paradise, The World of the Hudson River School*, New York: The Metropolitan Museum of Art, 1987, pp. 81-82.
9. Daingerfield, "Sketch of his Life," p. 1.
10. Charles C. Eldredge, *American Imagination and Symbolist Painting*, New York: Grey Art Gallery, 1979, pp. 36-37.

11. Ibid., p. 43.

12. Robert Hobbs, *Elliott Daingerfield*, p. 20.

13. Elizabeth Broun, *Albert Pinkham Ryder*, Washington, D.C.: The Smithsonian Institution Press, 1989, pp. 108, 165 and 174-175. This exhibition served as a milestone in Ryder scholarship and brought together, for the first time in recent museum history, a significant range of the artist's fragile works.

14. Ibid., pp. 33-35.

15. Barbara Novak, *American Painting of the Nineteenth Century*, New York: Praeger Publishers, 1969, p. 211.

16. Elliott Daingerfield, "Albert Pinkham Ryder, Artist and Dreamer," *Scribner's Magazine*, LXIII (March, 1918), p. 381.

17. Robert Hobbs, *Elliott Daingerfield*, p. 26.

18. Elliott Daingerfield, "Albert Pinkham Ryder," p. 384.

19. The nature of this painting invites variations in the interpretation of the central figures. Charles Eldredge, writing in *American Imagination and Symbolist Painting*, indicates that the figures are mother and child: "Mortality as a passage was also explored by Daingerfield in his *Mystic Brim*, of 1893, in which mother and child stand, attended by an angel, at the brink of the unknown, while about them swirl blond forms suggestive of angels and spirits." (p. 101). Bruce Chambers, in *Art and Artists of the South*, writes: "Daingerfield's first wife died in childbirth in 1891, and *Mystic Brim* of 1893 almost certainly interprets that event, portraying as it does both the artist and his wife, accompanied by an angel, standing upon a precipice looking out towards the heavens where seraphim swirl in chorus, (p. 71). A close examination of the painting shows that the central figure is rather androgynous and the smaller figure, also wrapped in classical robes, is unusually elongated and seems to have legs and a torso too large for the small, immature head. While it may be that the artist intended that these figures be purely allegorical, it does seem more likely that they represent the mother and (rather grown) child. A recent examination of a watercolor study for the painting, now in the possession of Duncan Connelly in Atlanta, reinforces the reading of the figures as mother and child.

20. On file in the Center for the Study of Southern Painting, Daingerfield Papers. Also, quoted in Bruce Chambers, *Art and Artists of the South*, p. 71.

21. Robert Goldwater, *Symbolism*, New York: Harper and Row, Publishers, 1979, pp. 116-117.

22. Charles Eldredge, *American Imagination and Symbolist Painting*, p. 15.

23. Ibid., p. 24.

24. Ibid., p. 16.

25. Ibid., pp. 20-21.

26. Richard Murray, "Painting and Sculpture," p. 181.

27. Ibid., p. 185.

28. Robert Hobbs, *Elliott Daingerfield*, p. 26.

29. Bruce Chambers, *Art and Artists of the South*, p. 83.

30. Ibid., p. 71. Also see Hobbs, p. 22.

31. Quoted in Estill Curtis Pennington, *A Southern Collection*, Augusta: Morris Communications Corporation, 1992, p. 92.

32. Elliott Daingerfield, "Nature vs. Art," *Scribner's Magazine*, XLIX, (February, 1911), p. 255.

33. Rick Stewart, "Toward a New South: The Regionalist Approach, 1900 to 1950," in *Painting in the South: 1564-1980*, Richmond: Virginia Museum, 1983, p. 106.

34. Nina Spalding Stevens, "Pilgrimage to the Artist's Paradise," *Fine Arts Journal*, February 1911 Number, p. 108. Nina Spalding Stevens is also listed in this article as the Assistant Director of the Toledo Art Museum.

35. Ibid., pp. 109-110.

36. "Souvenir of a journey to the Grand Canyon of Arizona," Chicago: Fine Arts Journal Press, undated, no pagination. Included in the Daingerfield files at the Center for the Study of Southern Painting.

37. Ibid.

38. Sandra D'Emilio and Suzan Campbell, *Visions & Visionaries, The Art & Artists of the Santa Fe Railway*, Salt Lake City: Peregrine Smith Books, 1991, pp. 9-16.

39. Nina Spalding Stevens, "Pilgrimage to the Artist's Paradise," p. 112.

40. Ibid., pp. 107, 112.

41. Ibid., p. 111.

42. Elliott Daingerfield, "Sketch of his Life," p. 2.

43. Robert Hobbs, *Elliott Daingerfield*, p. 46.

44. Sandra D'Emilio and Suzan Campbell, *Visions & Visionaries*, p. 65. This exhibition was presented at the Museum of Fine Arts, Museum of New Mexico in 1991.

45. Elliott Daingerfield, "Sketch of his Life," p. 2.

46. Ibid., p. 2.

47. From Daingerfield files at the Center for the Study of Southern Painting.

48. Ibid. Also in Charles Eldredge, *American Imagination and Symbolist Painting*, p. 145.

49. Ibid.

50. See Charles Eldredge, *American Imagination and Symbolist Painting*, p. 24. For additional information on the Armory Show and its importance in the development of American art, see Milton W. Brown, *The Story of the Armory Show*, New York: Abbeville Press, 1988. Redon was given the most favorable attention in press coverage of the exhibition. His works also sold exceptionally well: thirteen paintings and pastels and twenty prints were sold from the exhibition. See pp. 134-135.

51. Ibid., p. 81.

52. Ibid., p. 55.

53. Elliott Daingerfield, "Sketch of his Life," p. 3.

54. Ibid., p. 3.

55. See Anderson Galleries, *The Forum Exhibition of Modern American Painters*, New York: The Anderson Galleries, 1916; Reprint Edition, New York: Arno Press, 1968.

56. Elliott Daingerfield, "George Inness," *Century*, XCV (November, 1917), p. 71. For additional information on Inness, and Daingerfield's perspective on the artist, see *George Inness: The Man and His Art*, New York: Frederick Fairchild Sherman, 1911.

57. Kenyon Cox quoted in Richard Murray, "Painting and Sculpture," pp. 188-189.

58. Michael Kammen, *Mystic Chords of Memory*, p. 99.

59. Ibid.

60. Robert Hobbs, *Elliott Daingerfield*, p. 50.

61. Rick Stewart, "Toward a New South," p. 106.

62. Michael Kammen, *Mystic Chords of Memory*, p. 101. See also Estill Curtis Pennington, "Ruin and Remembrance," in *Look Away, Reality and Sentiment in Southern Art*, Spartanburg: Saraland Press, 1989, pp. 149-183.

63. Elliott Daingerfield, "Sketch of his Life," p. 3.

THE COLLECTION

1885	**Priest Holding a Dead Duck**
	Watercolor on paper
	11 x 7 inches
	1993.C0916
1885	**Dull Times**
	Oil on canvas
	18 x 14 inches
	1993.C1039
1886	**Chrysanthemums in a Devil Vase**
	Oil on canvas
	34 x 24 inches
	1989.01.048
1887	**Return at Twilight**
	Oil on canvas
	28⅛ x 48⅛ inches
	1989.01.047
1887	**Steeplechase**
	Oil on canvas
	7 x 9⅛ inches
	1989.01.050
1890	**Self Portrait**
	Oil on canvas
	28⅛ x 24 1/16 inches
	1993.C0313
before 1892	**Study for the Harvest**
	Graphite on paperboard
	7 x 4½ inches
	1993.C0890

1893   The Mystic Brim
Oil on canvas
29¾ x 36 inches.
1989.01.038

c. 1891-1895   Study for "Grief"
Oil on board
9⅞ x 12 inches
1993.C0949

c. 1891-1895   Grief
Oil on canvasboard
32 x 40⅛ inches
1993.C0319

c. 1894   Head of a Mountain Woman
Graphite on paper
15 x 11 inches
1989.01.049

1895   Mysterious Night
Watercolor on board
30½ x 21½ inches
1989.01.043

1890-1910   Flight into Egypt
Watercolor on paper
16½ x 20½ inches
1993.C0253

1890-1910   Madonna and Child in Courtyard
Oil on canvas
12 x 20 inches
1989.01.040

1890-1910   Milk Maid
Oil on canvas
24 x 34 inches
1989.01.041

before 1900   Study of Bulls
Chalk on board
10⅞ x 13⅞ inches
1993.C0912

before 1900   Study of Trees
Charcoal on blue paper
12⅞ x 9½ inches
1993.C0959

c. 1900   Study of Marjorie for the Study of the Madonna
Graphite on paper
7½ x 15½ inches
1993.C0626

1900-1905   Portrait of Ben Fosdick
Charcoal on blue paper
21 x 15 inches
1993.C0947

1900-1910   Helen McCarthy
Charcoal and chalk on blue paperboard
23⅞ x 17 inches
1993.C0886

1902-1905   Charity - Nude Study
Graphite on paper
11¾ x 15½ inches
1993.C0940

1902-1905	Balthazar - Drapery Study		1902-1905	Melchior - Nude Study
	Graphite on pape			*Graphite on paper*
	12½ x 10 inches			14½ x 11 inches
	1993.C0844			1993.C0938
1902-1905	Cherub		1902-1905	Soldier - Drapery Study
	Graphite on paper			*Graphite and charcoal on paper*
	15 x 13 inches			14 x 17 ¼ inches
	1993.C0920			1993.C0945
1902-1905	Cherub with Hammer		1902-1905	St. Anne - Drapery Study
	Graphite on paper			*Graphite on paper*
	10½ x 11 inches			18¼ x 13 inches
	1993.C0960			1993.C0941
1902-1905	Faith - Drapery Study		c. 1902-1906	Figure of the Virgin Mary - Drapery Study
	Graphite on paper			*Graphite on paper mounted on board*
	18 x 14 inches			19 x 15 inches
	1993.C0881			1993.C0625
1902-1905	Figure of a Man - Drapery Study		c. 1902-1906	Seated Soldier
	Graphite on paper			*Graphite on paper*
	17 x 13 inches			15¾ x 12 inches
	1993.C0922			1993.C0937
1902-1905	Gaspar - Nude Study		1902-1906	Archangel Gabriel - Drapery Study
	Graphite on paper			*Graphite on paper*
	16 x 12 inches			19 x 15 inches
	1993.C0939			1993.C0936
1902-1905	Gaspar - Drapery Study		1902-1906	Archangel Michael - Nude Study A
	Graphite on paper			*Graphite on paper*
	19 x 14 inches			18 x 14½ inches
	1993.C0921			1993.C0888

1902-1906   Archangel Michael - Nude Study B
Graphite on paper
19½ x 15½ inches
1993.C0919

1902-1906   Archangel Michael - Armor and Drapery Study
Graphite on paper
19⅞ x 15¾ inches
1993.C0925

1902-1906   Sketch of a Seated Woman
Graphite on paper
17¼ x 13½ inches
1993.C0882

1902-1906   St. Catherine - Drapery Study
Graphite on paperboard
14⅞ x 17⅞ inches
1993.C0930

1902-1906   St. Cecilia - Drapery Study
Graphite on paper
18 x 14 inches
1993.C0935

1902-1906   St. Cecilia - Study of Head
Graphite on paper
21 x 15¾ inches
1993.C0946

1902-1906   St. George - Nude Study
Graphite on paper
19½ x 12 inches
1993.C0932

1902-1906   St. John the Evangelist - Drapery Study
Graphite on paper
19 x 14 inches
1993.C0943

1902-1906   St. Paul - Nude Study
Graphite on paper
19 x 15 inches
1993.C0944

1902-1906   St. Stephen - Drapery Study
Graphite on paper
19½ x 10½
1993.C0931

1902-1906   Study of Brocade
Graphite on paper
15 x 11 inches
1993.C0883

1902-1906   Priest - Drapery Study
Graphite on paper
19 x 14 inches
1993.C0924

1902-1906   Priest - Nude Study
Graphite on paper
19½ x 14½ inches
1993.C0934

1905-1910   Christ Stilling the Tempest
Oil on canvas
20 x 24 inches
1989.01.046

1910   Grandfather Mountain, N.C.
Watercolor on paper
9 x 12¼ inches
1989.01.044

1910-1920   Grandfather Mountain, N.C.
Watercolor on paper
9¼ x 13¼ inches
1993.C0176

1912   A Fantasy, 1912
Oil on canvas
28 x 24 inches
1993.C0734

early 20th cen. Golden Moon
Oil on canvas
6 x 8⅛ inches
1989.01.042

1910-1915   Marjorie in Valentine Costume
Oil on canvas
25 x 18 inches
1993.C0347

1911-1913   Grand Canyon #2
Oil on board
10 x 8 inches
1993.C0179

1911-1915   Study for "Call of the Winds"
Graphite on paper
12⅝ x 11½ inches
1993.C0933

c. 1913-1915   The Lone Cypress
Oil on canvas
30¼ x 36¼ inches
1993.C0695

c. 1913-1915   Neptune's Daughter
Oil on canvas
24 x 34¼ inches
1993.C0735

1913   The Genius of the Canyon
Oil on canvas
36 x 48½ inches
1989.01.039

c. 1913-1914   Study for "The Sleepers"
Graphite on paper
12⅜ x 16¼ inches
1993.C0927

1914   The Sleepers, 1914
Oil on canvas mounted on board
36 x 48⅛ inches
1993.C0814

c. 1915   Carolina Sunlight
Oil on canvas
24 x 28¼ inches
1989.01.045

c. 1915   Sunset Glory
Oil on canvas
27½ x 33¾ inches
1990.014

c. 1917   Westglow
Oil on board
12 x 16 inches
1993.CXX08

no date   The Artist's Mother
Graphite on paperboard
15½ x 11¼ inches
1993.C0905

no date   Bathers at a Stream
Pastel on gray paper
7½ x 10 inches
1993.C0951

no date   Black Lady Leaning Against a Rock
Pastel on paper
8¾ x 8½ inches
1993.C1024

no date   Cherub and Nude Lady
Ink on paper on board
7¼ x 10 inches
1993.C0889

no date   Christ - Resurrection
Graphite on paper
14¾ x 8¾ inches
1993.C0899

no date   Double Landscape with Figure Sketch
Graphite on paper
9¾ x 7¼ inches
1993.C0897

no date

Girl with Drapery
Graphite on paperboard
11¼ x 8½ inches
1993.C0907

no date

Hand Holding Hat - Study
Graphite on paper
15½ x 11½ inches
1993.C0942

no date

Hanging Grapes
Watercolor on paper
18⅜ x 21⅞ inches
1993.C0887

no date

Head Studies of a Lady
Charcoal on paper
9¾ x 14¾ inches
1993.C0906

no date

Head Study of a Lady
Pastel on gray paper
9¾ x 7½ inches
1993.C0958

no date

Heavenly Musicians
Pastel on paper
7⅜ x 9⅜ inches
1993.C0918

no date

Infant with Drapery
Pastel on paper
7¾ x 6½ inches
1993.C0709

no date

Kneeling Man - Nude Study
Graphite on paperboard
15¼ x 9¾ inches
1993.C0928

no date

Lady with Flower - Nude Study
Graphite on paperboard
15⅞ x 11⅞ inches
1993.C0895

no date

Landscape
Pastel on brown paperboard
6⅜ x 7½ inches
1993.C0914

no date
Landscape - Hillside House
Pastel on gray paper
5½ x 8¼ inches
1993.C1022

no date
Landscape - Orange Sky and Water
Pastel on gray paper
7 x 8⅛ inches
1993.C0957

no date
Landscape - Sunset I
Pastel on paper
5¼ x 7⅞ inches
1993.C0708

no date
Landscape - Sunset II
Pastel on gray paper
7 x 8⅞ inches
1993.C0961

no date
Landscape with Houses
Graphite on paper
4 x 6½ inches
1993.C0952

no date
Landscape with Stream
Graphite on paper
8½ x 12¾ inches
1993.C0103

no date
Madonna and Child
Graphite on paper
16 x 12 inches
1993.C0885

no date
Madonna and Child and Wise Men
Graphite on paper
7⅝ x 10⅞ inches
1993.C0954

no date
Multiple Sketches: Woman's Head and Symbolist Figures
Graphite on paper
9¾ x 14½ inches
1993.C0901

no date
Nocturne - Moon and Surf
Watercolor on paper
7⅝ x 10⅞ inches
1993.C1507

no date — **Nude Beach View - On Drapery**
Graphite on paper
9½ x 7⅞ inches
1993.C0929

no date — **Nude Study of a Woman**
Graphite and charcoal on paperboard
19⅞ x 13¾ inches
1993.C0911

no date — **Ocean Study**
Pastel on black paperboard
7¾ x 9¾ inches
1993.C0915

no date — **Reclining Nude, Back View, and Lady with Pot**
Graphite on paper
8¼ x 11¼ inches
1993.C0926

no date — **Seated Woman - Nude Study**
Graphite on paper
15½ x 10⅞ inches
1993.C0892

no date — **Sketch - Figures on a Beach**
Charcoal and crayon on paper
9¾ x 15¾ inches
1993.C0913

no date — **Sketch - Hand Studies and a Plant**
Graphite on paper
9¼ x 13⅞ inches
1993.C0900

no date   Sketch: Hand Study and Man with a Goat
Graphite on paper
9¾ x 15¼ inches
1993.C0904

no date   Sketch - Head of a Lady
Charcoal on paper
22½ x 16 inches
1993.C0923

no date   Sketch: Mother and Child, and Arm Study
Graphite on paper
9¾ x 15¾ inches
1993.C0902

no date   Sketch of a Lady
Graphite on paper
10 x 8 inches
1993.C0891

no date   Sketch of a Seated Lady and Two Symbolist Figure Sketches
Graphite on paper
15¼ x 9¾ inches
1993.C0903

no date   Sketch of Trees
Graphite on paper
9¾ x 15¾ inches
1993.C1508

no date   Sketch of Two Trees
Graphite on paperboard
9 x 6 inches
1993.C0569

no date   Sketch - Symbolist Figures
Graphite on paper
4½ x 5¼ inches
1993.C0896

no date   Sketches - Monk, Seated Woman and Cherub and Owls
Graphite on blue paperboard
14¼ x 10¼ inches
1993.C0908

no date   Standing Man - Nude Study
Graphite on paper
14⅜ x 9¾ inches
1993.C0893

no date   Study of a Young Lady
Charcoal and white chalk on blue paper
22 x 16 inches
1993.C0966

no date   Study of Christ Child
Graphite on paper
5¾ x 8 inches
1993.C0544

no date   Symbolist Sketch with Figures
Graphite on paperboard, mounted on board
9⅞ x 16 inches
1993.C0909

no date   Woman Seated - Nude Study
Graphite on paper
9⅞ x 7⅜ inches
1993.C0894

no date   Young Child Playing with Toys
Pastel on gray paper
7⅜ x 6⅛ inches
1993.C0962

INDEX of ILLUSTRATIONS

p. 2   Neptune's Daughter, *c. 1913-1915*
Oil on canvas, 24 x 34 ¼ inches, 1993.C0735

p. 6   Elliott Daingerfield and his daughter, Marjorie. *(Undated photograph). CSSP.*

p. 9   Elliott Daingerfield in his library. *(Undated photograph). CSSP.*

p. 10   Kenyon Cox – Portrait of Elliott Daingerfield, *Feb. 24, 1890*
Oil on canvas 20 x 16 inches 1993.C0079

p. 16   *Illustration 1* – Self Portrait, *c. 1890*
Oil on canvas, 28⅛ x 24 1/16 inches, 1993.C0313

p. 18   *Illustration 2* – Lady with Flower - Nude Study, *no date*
Graphite on paperboard, 15⅞ x 11⅞ inches, 1993.C0895

p. 20   *Illustration 3* – Archangel Michael - Nude Study B, *1902-1906*
Graphite on paper, 19½ x 15½ inches, 1993.C0919

p. 21   *Illustration 4* – Chrysanthemums in a Devil Vase , *1886*
Oil on canvas, 34 x 24 inches, 1989.01.048

p. 22   *Illustration 5* – Return at Twilight, *1887*
Oil on canvas, 28⅛ x 48⅛ inches, 1989.01.047

p. 23   *Illustration 6* – Milk Maid, *late 19th/early 20th century*
Oil on canvas, 24 x 34 inches, 1989.01.041

p. 23   *Illustration 7* – Steeplechase, *1887*
Oil on canvas, 7 x 9⅛ inches, 1989.01.050

p. 24   *Illustration 8* – Christ Stilling the Tempest, *1905-10*
Oil on canvas, 20 x 24 inches, 1989.01.046

p. 26   *Illustration 9* – The Mystic Brim , *1893*
Oil on canvas, 29¾ x 36 inches, 1989.01.038

p. 28   *Illustration 10* – Epiphany, *1905*
Mural, In the Lady Chapel of St. Mary the Virgin, New York City, New York.

p. 29   *Illustration 11* – Archangel Michael - Armor and Drapery Study for Magnificat
1902-1906, Graphite on paper, 19⅜ x 15 ¾ inches, 1993.C0925

p. 30   *Illustration 12* – Mysterious Night, *1895*
Watercolor on board, 30½ x 21½ inches, 1989.01.043

p. 31   *Illustration 13* – Grandfather Mountain, N.C., *1910*
Watercolor on paper, 9 x 12¼ inches, 1989.01.044

p. 32   *Illustration 14* – Grandfather Mountain, N.C., *1910*
         Watercolor on paper, 9¼ x 13¼ inches, 1993.C0176

p. 32   A view from the balcony of Westglow, *(Undated photograph). CSSP.*

p. 33   *Illustration 15* – Sunset Glory, *c. 1915*
         Oil on canvas, 27½ x 33¾ inches, 1990.014

p. 34   *Illustration 16* – Carolina Sunlight, *c. 1915*
         Oil on canvas, 24 x 28¼ inches, 1989.01.045

p. 37   *Illustration 17* – Grand Canyon #2, *c. 1911-1913*
         Oil on board, 10 x 8 inches, 1993.C0179

p. 38   *Illustration 18* – The Lifting Veil, *1913*
         Oil on canvas, 32 x 48 inches,
         Courtesy of the Santa Fe Railway, Schaumburg, Illinois

p. 39   *Illustration 19* – The Lone Cypress, *c. 1913-1915*
         Oil on canvas, 30¼ x 36¼ inches, 1993.C0695

p. 40   *Illustration 20* – The Genius of the Canyon, *1913*
         Oil on canvas, 36 x 48½ inches, 1989.01.039

p. 42   *Illustration 21* – The Sleepers, *1914*
         Oil on canvas mounted on board, 36 x 48½ inches, 1993.C0814

p. 43   *Illustration 22* – Study for "The Sleepers," *c. 1913-1914*
         Graphite on paper, 12⅜ x 16¾ inches, 1993.C0927

p. 44   *Illustration 23* – Spirit of the Storm, *1912*
         Oil on canvas mounted on board, 36 x 48⅛ inches
         Courtesy of Reynolda House, Museum of American Art Winston-Salem, N.C.

p. 46   Westglow, Blowing Rock North Carolina. *(Undated photograph,*
         1916 or later). CSSP.

p. 47   *Illustration 24* – Westglow, *c. 1917*
         Oil on board, 12 x 16 inches, 1993.CXX08

p. 49   A Dream of Venice, *c. 1924*
         30 x 36 inches (Undated photograph of painting). CSSP.

p. 53   Christ – Resurrection, *no date*
         Graphite on paper, 14¼ x 8¾ inches, 1993.C0899

p. 54   Nude Study of a Woman, *no date*
         Graphite and charcoal on paperboard 19⅞ x 13¾ inches, 1993.C0911

p. 57   Elliott Daingerfield and students, *(Undated photograph). CSSP.*

p. 58   Uncaptioned photograph. Elliott Daingerfield, and members of the
         National Academy of Design *(?). CSSP.*

p. 60   The Artist's Mother, *no date*
         Graphite on paperboard 15½ x 11¼ inches 1993.C0905

p. 61   Uncaptioned photograph. The artist's mother *(?) (1898) CSSP.*

p. 62   The artist's model, Marjorie Daingerfield *(?) (Undated photograph). CSSP.*

p. 63   Marjorie in Valentine Costume, *1910-1915*
         Oil on canvas, 25 x 18 inches 1993. C0347

p. 64   Elliott Daingerfiled and students. *(Undated photograph). CSSP.*

p. 65   Elliott Daingerfield at ease on the porch of Wynnwood
         Blowing Rock, North Carolina. *(Undated photograph). CSSP.*

p. 67   Elliott Daingerfield in the studio at work on Grand Canyon painting. *April 1911*
         From the collection of Mr. and Mrs. Joseph Dulaney.

p. 68   Elliott Daingerfield with Anna Daingerfield (first figure, foreground) and party at
         the Grand Canyon. *November, 1910.*
         From the collection of Mr. and Mrs. Joseph Dulaney.

p. 69   Grand Canyon (from the artist's sketchbook), *c. 1910*
         Pencil on paper, 7¾ x 5¼ inches
         From the collection of Mr. and Mrs. Joseph Dulaney.

ABOUT THE AUTHORS

ESTILL CURTIS PENNINGTON was educated at the University of Kentucky, the University of Georgia, and in the Smithsonian Institution Ph. D. program at George Washington University. Prior to his association with the Morris Museum of Art as Curator of Southern Painting, he worked with the National Portrait Gallery and the Archives of American Art at the Smithsonian. He also has served as Director of the Lauren Rogers Museum of Art and as Curator of Painting at the New Orleans Museum of Art. He is widely acknowledged as one of the leading authorities on the art of the South, and has written numerous exhibition catalogues, articles and books in the field.

J. RICHARD GRUBER is Deputy Director of the Morris Museum of Art and Director of the Museum's Center for the Study of Southern Painting. He holds the M. A. degree in the History of Art from the University of Colorado and the Ph. D. in the History of Art from the University of Kansas. As an art historian, he has concentrated on American art and design of the 20th century. Prior to joining the Morris Museum of Art, he was Director of the Memphis Brooks Museum of Art in Tennessee, Director of the Wichita Art Museum in Kansas, and Director of the Peter Joseph Gallery in New York.